Between the Bible and the Church

Between the Bible

the Bible

and the Church

New Methods for
Biblical Preaching

David L. Bartlett

Abingdon Press
Nashville

BETWEEN THE BIBLE AND THE CHURCH
NEW METHODS FOR BIBLICAL PREACHING

This book is printed on acid-free paper.

Library of Congress Cataloging-in-Publication Data

Bartlett, David Lyon, 1941-
  Between the Bible and the church : new methods for biblical preaching / David L. Bartlett.
      p.   cm.
    ISBN 0-687-02825-6 (alk. paper)
    1. Bible—Homiletical use.   I. Title
  BS534.5.B36   1999
  251—dc21   98-31140
                                                                              CIP

Scripture quotations, unless otherwise noted, are from the New Revised Standard Version of the Bible. Copyright © 1989 by the Division of Christian Education of the National Council of the Churches of Christ in the United States of America. All rights reserved.

Publishers have given permission to use extended quotations from the following copyrighted works:

The First Urban Christians: The Social World of the Apostle Paul, by Wayne A. Meeks. Copyright 1983 Yale University Press. Reprinted by permission of publisher.

Luke (Westminster Bible Companion Series). Copyright 1995 Sharon H. Ringe. Used by permission of Westminster John Knox Press.

Reading from This Place vol. 2, edited by Fernando F. Segovia and Mary Ann Tolbert. Copyright 1995 Augsburg Fortress. Reprinted by permission of publisher.

Slavery as Salvation: The Metaphor of Slavery in Pauline Christianity, by Dale Martin. Copyright 1990 Yale University Press. Reprinted by permission of publisher.

Treasures New and Old: Contributions to Matthean Studies (SBL Symposium Series), edited by David R. Bauer and Mark Alan Powell. Ulrich Luz, "The Final Judgment (Matt. 25:31-46): An Exercise in 'History of Influence' Exegesis." Copyright 1996 Scholars Press. Reprinted by permission of publisher and Luz.

99 00 01 02 03 04 05 06 07 08—10 9 8 7 6 5 4 3 2 1

MANUFACTURED IN THE UNITED STATES OF AMERICA

For Benjamin and Jonah, with love

Contents

A c k n o w l e d g m e n t s

This book is the culmination of a long process of reflecting, writing, and lecturing on the relationship between biblical studies and preaching. In writing this material, I drew on a variety of classes and discussions—a graduate seminar on biblical hermeneutics at Yale University; a series of presentations and discussions at the "Interpreting the Faith" conference at Union Seminary in Virginia; discussions at the research fellows seminar and at the faculty forum at Yale Divinity School; and an informal discussion with Presbyterian clergy gathered at Westover Hills Presbyterian Church in Little Rock.

A number of friends have responded to my queries with bibliographical suggestions and helps in clarifying my discussion. I want to note in particular the generous response of Brevard Childs to my questions about the implications of canonical interpretation of the Bible.

Some of the material in this book was presented in diverse forms as the MacLeod Lectures at Princeton Theological Seminary, the Jameson Jones Lectures at Duke University Divinity School, and the Westervelt Lectures at Austin Presbyterian Theological Seminary.

I am grateful to the friends, both old and new, who extended such wonderful hospitality on each of those occasions. I know the other friends will understand if I add a particular word of thanks to Jack and Virginia Stotts of Austin, whose kindness on the occasion of the lectures was one more in a long series of graces extended to my family and me.

Carol, Benjamin, and Jonah Bartlett provide the joy that sustains my work.

This book grows out of an enduring conviction. Right preaching is the interpretation of Scripture. There is much excellent Christian speech that is not preaching. Christians, even Christian preachers, entertain, inform, inspire, and opine. Often these presentations help the faithful and edify the community, but they are not preaching. They are not what every congregation has a right to expect when its members wait for the preacher to preach. The sermon may be a carefully constructed oration or an apparently less formal conversation; it may consist mostly of stories or mostly of word studies; it may draw deeply from the experience of the preacher or deeply from the theological tradition of the denomination, but unless it is an interpretation of the text or texts that the congregation has just heard read aloud, it is not preaching.

In the penultimate chapter of this book, I will claim that every interpretation of Scripture and, finally, every theological claim reveal something of the standpoint of the interpreter. Legend has it that Martin Luther began the Protestant Reformation both by his attention to Scripture and by his personal confession: "Here I stand. God help me; I can do no other."

It seems only fair, therefore, that I include here a word about standpoint—where I stand.

When I began my seminary career at Yale Divinity School in 1963, that school, like many other theological institutions, lived very much under the shadow of Karl Barth—like many shadows, sometimes comforting and sometimes threatening. In those years, I was convicted perhaps forever of the rightness of Barth's early claim. God's word comes to us in three forms.[1] First and foremost, God's word is incarnate in Jesus Christ, and it is in Jesus Christ that God works redemption for us and for the whole creation. Second, God's word comes to us in the

Bible, not because God dictated the Bible word for word, but because the Bible—Old Testament and New—testifies, as testaments should, to Jesus Christ. At his most Barthian, Barth lifts the authority of Scripture for preaching to awesome heights: "Scriptural exegesis rests on the assumption that the message which Scripture has to give us, even in its apparently most debatable and least assimilable parts, is in all circumstances truer and more important than the best and most necessary things that we ourselves have said or can say."[2]

That is to say that Leviticus 24:5-9 and the entire book of Jude are truer and more important than Augustine's *Confessions* or Bonhoeffer's *Letters and Papers from Prison* or Teresa of Avila's *The Interior Castle*.

The third form of the word of God is preaching. Preaching's authority is not derived from itself, the call of the preacher, or the authority of the church, but from Jesus Christ, who is proclaimed by preaching. For Barth, of course, we do not reach Christ apart from Scripture—not through nature or history or our own experience. The third form of the word of God presupposes the second form. We preach the crucified Christ through Scripture because Scripture is where we find the cross held high.

Nothing in my thirty some years of preaching has shaken my conviction that Barth is here a faithful witness. To be sure, Scriptural preaching can be picky and dull; to be sure, the prophets preached not texts, but living oracles; and the apostles preached the testimony of the crucified Christ, though it was not yet written down. But I am neither prophet nor apostle, and the words that bear witness to their witness are contained between the covers of my Bible. Preaching lives under the promise that, where the Word is faithfully and carefully interpreted, God still speaks to God's people. If that is not true, we can open theological academies or religious entertainment centers because church is over and done.

Thomas Long, whose book *The Witness of Preaching* classifies Barthians, if not Barth, as those who believe the preacher to be a herald declaring a kerygma not our own, points us toward a more nuanced view of the preacher as witness. "We go to Scripture . . . not to glean a set of facts about God or the faith . . . but to encounter a presence, to hear God's voice speaking to us ever anew."[3] This is a wise corrective to what I think is a misreading of Barth that makes it sound as if preaching is always once removed from its subject. We sometimes preach the Bible and pretend the Bible preaches Christ, as if we were part of some halfway covenant declaring a faith that our forebears lived and we only remember. Barth likened the preacher to John the Baptist pointing to the one greater than he. Though we use the Bible, we do not preach so that people may encounter the Bible, but so that people may encounter Christ.

Some years after graduating from Yale, I went to teach at the Divinity School of the University of Chicago. There, for the first time I read Hans Georg Gadamer's *Truth and Method* and heard David Tracy interpret Gadamer for his students.[4] Gadamer insists that every interpretation, even every interpretation of Scripture, is a conversation. We do not come to any text without questions, presuppositions, or history. Truth is, I needed Gadamer to give me a structure for what I already had discovered. By the time I read Gadamer I had been preaching weekly for about ten years, and had discovered that whatever theory of preaching we may want to maintain, all of us can confess empirically. I had preached very different sermons based on careful study of the same text. The sermons were refracted through the experience of preacher and congregation in very different ways. Sometimes the different sermons proved to be helpful, (relatively) faithful expositions of a true but wonderfully multifaceted word.

I am still Barthian enough to add to Gadamer that, when we are in conversation with Scripture, Scripture is still the senior partner in that conversation. For me, Scripture functions rather as the Creator functions for Job. The end of the conversation often goes like this: "Who is this that darkens counsel by words without knowledge? Gird up your loins like a man. I will question you, and you shall declare to me" (Job 38:2-3). Of course, as sovereign and free as God is in this passage, it is perhaps worth noting that God was at last enticed to break the silence by Job's incessant insistence on being part of the cosmic conversation.

Nor is Barth unaware of the extent to which perspective shapes our interpretation and preaching.

> [When we as interpreters subordinate ourselves to God's Word], it is not as though we had simply to abandon our ideas, thoughts, and convictions. We certainly cannot do that, just as little as we can free ourselves from our own shadow. Nor should we try to do it; for that would be arrogance rather than humility. . . . It cannot mean that we have to allow our ideas, thoughts, and convictions to be supplanted, so to speak, by those of the prophets and apostles, or that we have to begin to speak the language of Canaan instead of our own tongue. In that case, we should not have subordinated ourselves to them but, at most, adorned ourselves with their feathers. In that case, nothing would have been done in the interpretation of their words, for we should merely have repeated them parrot-like. . . . Subordination, if it is to be sincere, must concern the purpose and meaning indicated in the ideas, thoughts, and convictions of the prophets and apostles; that is, the testimony which, by what they say as human beings like ourselves, they wish to bear.[5]

And, of course, to read Barth's sermons is to hear a voice deeply grounded in the issues of his time and profoundly aware of the questions and circumstances of his congregation.

Nonetheless, Robert Clyde Johnson, who taught theology at Yale for many years, often said that he did theology like Barth, but preached like Paul Tillich. We know what he means: when the time comes to preach, the Word does sometimes seem a little naked for mortal eyes to gaze upon. Connections help, and if that is a concession to our mortality, it is not the first concession the Godhead has made to our weakness, nor the most important one. This is part of what Long helps us see with his image of the witness.

Of course while teaching and preaching in Chicago and later in Oakland and Richmond, I kept reading works by faculty members at Yale. While I do not believe there really is something called a Yale School, I did go to school at Yale and now teach there, and one cannot be there long without paying some attention to Hans Frei. Frei's major work *The Eclipse of Biblical Narrative* is, first of all, a historical study of biblical interpretation, not a proposal for our interpreting, though, as in much of the most interesting history, the proposal is not far beneath the surface.

Frei suggests that twentieth-century biblical interpretation has gone awry because we have separated narrative from history, the story from the facts. Fundamentalists insist that the narrative is an accurate description of generally available facts: that is the way it happened. Liberals tend to insist that the narrative is in danger of obscuring the facts: that is *not* the way it happened, but if we can get behind the text we can find out what really did happen, probably to our edification. You know how it goes: the Gospels say Jesus multiplied the loaves and fishes; but getting behind the text, we can see that our Lord inspired generosity among all those Galileans who had been hoarding supper in their hampers. By the turn of the century, Frei says, "The choice of subject matter finally came to be between the two extremes of literally intended accounts, which are reliable factual reports, and historically understood mythical accounts, which have no essential connection with fact reporting."[6]

Frei's suggestion is that the proper way to interpret biblical narrative is not to look at the history behind the narrative, nor at the intention of a real or implied author, nor at any kind of separate subject matter, but to look at the narrative itself. For Frei, both in this book and elsewhere, the Gospels in particular are those compelling narratives that represent and re-present Jesus

Christ in such a way as to confront us not just with the story but with its hero.[7] My reading of the strengths and some of the limitations of Frei's understanding will get clearer, I hope, as we talk about the relationship between narrative and historical-critical readings of Scripture text. But at the beginning of this study I confess that Frei has helped me to wean myself from earlier obsessive questing for the historical Jesus or the real exodus, and to give greater attention and loyalty to the Jesus the Gospels portray and the exodus the Pentateuch celebrates.

Here is what we find as we consider the relationship of preaching to the biblical texts: The Bible provides the source and the criterion of faithful preaching. Sermons start with texts; however, preaching is not just a matter of reading the Scripture in a loud voice, or dramatically. New occasions demand new interpretations, shifted nuances, applications that our forebears never dreamed. The trick, or the gift, is to deal seriously with the text without attempting or pretending simply to replicate it.

Fortunately, Scripture itself provides a multitude of examples of doing just what preachers have to do: take a text or tradition and reshape it or reapply it to the issues of a new time, or the needs of a different community. That is to say that if we are to take the Bible absolutely seriously, we cannot take it as a bare and uninterpreted word. Scripture is not a matter of repetition so much as it is a matter of reappropriation. To be biblical prevents us from being biblicists. God may be the same yesterday, today, and tomorrow, but words about God shift, even in the Bible.

Not only does the example or Scripture provide us with a warrant for doing what we have to do—interpret—it provides us with a number of models of how we might do it.

Let me describe several such models and in each case dare to say how the scriptural writers might provide models for preaching types to which we are antitypes.

The archetype for this interpretive task is the scribe Jesus praises in Matthew 13:52. "Therefore every scribe who has been trained for the kingdom of heaven is like the master of a household who brings out of his treasure what is new and what is old." Some have thought that Matthew was cleverly describing himself here. The author of Matthew's Gospel certainly brings forth out of his treasure what is new and what is old. The Old Testament is interpreted in the light of the new thing that has happened in Jesus Christ. Hence the so-called formula quotations: "And this happened in order that the scripture might be fulfilled which says. . . ." More recent "old things" are used as well, the Gospel of Mark and perhaps the elusive "Q" are brought together in a brand-new thing we call Matthew's Gospel. If that is right, Matthew warrants us to do brand-new things in our sermons, too— something old, something new, something borrowed. And Matthew was not the first scribe to understand his task that way.

I want to look at some of the ways in which Scripture interprets Scripture, and to use that analysis to provide clues for our own interpretation, our own preaching.

Echoes and Allusions

Richard Hays has provided an enticing study of the way in which Paul's Letters reflect the apostle's knowledge of Scripture—the Old Testament. The letters can be read "intertextually" because our texts reflect texts or sayings and stories that Paul knew.

For instance, Hays attends to Paul's use of a biblical image in Romans 9:19-24.

> You will say to me then, "Why then does [God] still find fault? For who can resist his will?" But who indeed are you, a human being, to argue with God? Will what is molded say to the one who molds it, "Why have you made me like this?" Has the potter no right over the clay, to make out of the same lump one object for special use and another for ordinary use? What if God, desiring to show his wrath and to make known his power, has

endured with much patience the objects of wrath that are made for destruction; and what if he has done so in order to make known the riches of his glory for the objects of mercy, which he has prepared beforehand for glory—including us whom he has called, not from the Jews only but also from the Gentiles?

Remember that Paul is here discussing God's dealing with both Gentiles and Jews in the whole economy of salvation. An imagined debate partner asks Paul how God, who chooses some to believe and some not, can possibly blame unbelievers whose destiny is not in their own hands. Paul responds with the image of the potter and the clay, and the image might be read to mean simply that God as creator has every right to do what God chooses with creation; if we are among the non-elect, we have no possible grounds for complaint.

However, there is an echo here of an Old Testament passage on potters and clay—Jeremiah 18:3-6: "So I went down to the potter's house, and there he was working at his wheel. The vessel he was making of clay was spoiled in the potter's hand, and he reworked it into another vessel, as seemed good to him. Then the word of the LORD came to me: Can I not do with you, O house of Israel, just as this potter has done? says the LORD. Just like the clay in the potter's hand, so are you in my hand, O house of Israel."

Here is how Hays explains the resonance of the Jeremiah allusion: "[The parable] resonates deeply with Paul's wider argument about God's dealings with Israel. The parable suggests that the potter's power is not destructive but creative: the vessel may fall, but the potter reshapes it. The parable, spoken in prophetic judgment upon Israel, is simultaneously a summons to repentance and a reassurance of the benevolent sovereignty of God. . . ."[8] Therefore, the image of the potter and the clay not only echoes Jeremiah, through Jeremiah it foreshadows the claim that Paul will make in Romans 11, that God has by no means abandoned Israel.

Hays finds here an explicit echo of the Old Testament. The preacher may find another echo which perhaps does not represent any planning on the part of Paul. The debate between Paul's imaginary questioner and God reminds us of Job's ongoing debate with God, and God's answer to Job's question: "Who are you, part of the creation, to argue with me, the Creator?" Yet, as Christians, we also can read Job in the light of Romans, or see in God's answer to Job what is really there but what Romans helps us see more clearly. God claims God's rights as Creator, not as superpower or cosmic thug. What God is about is the creation of a universe so full of beauty and delight that all the morning stars can sing together and the heavenly beings shout for joy. Allusion works forward and backward, too; in Romans 8:19-23, perhaps Job's God recalls the song for which the whole creation longs. Creation longs for the moment when Job's God restores the universe to song, when the divine potter fashions a vessel of beauty inestimable and enduring.

The use of allusion is evident elsewhere in the New Testament, too. Take John 3:16, which is the explicit text for many fine sermons and the implicit text for almost all of them: "For God so loved the world that he gave his only Son, so that everyone who believes in him may not perish but may have eternal life." The first readers or hearers of John's Gospel probably had grown up in the synagogue, and they would have heard echoes in this passage that we also hear.[9] Perhaps the loudest echo is that of Genesis 22:2: "Take your son, your only son Isaac, whom you love. . . ." Remembering that story, the early Christians who hear John 3:16 think back to the Genesis account, where Abraham speaks better than he knows in the immediate context of Genesis and far better than he could possibly know in the larger context of the Christian canon. Isaac cries: "Where is the lamb for a burnt offering?" Abraham responds: "God himself will provide the lamb for a burnt offering, my son" (Gen. 22:7-8). Now the listeners of John's Gospel think forward to that book again and to words heard not many verses before, the Baptist's witness to Jesus: "Here is the Lamb of God who takes away the sin of the world" (John 1:29).

(I wish the NRSV had kept the word *behold* because it captures better what John is saying: not just *Here is the lamb*, but *Look! here is the lamb*. Perhaps I also wish that translation because of my own echoes of the RSV, and before that the King James, which *sound* richer. Think of the way we use language. *Here's Anna* is not quite the same as *Look! it's Anna*. I do not like John 19:5 any better; Pilate says, "Here is the man," and we all know he means, "Behold the man!" Or at least, "Look! the man." John 19:5 echoes John 1:29, and will be echoed by John 19:37: "They will look on the one whom they have pierced." This is not just a word game. It is an attempt to point to the way that Scripture plays on Scripture, and that our preaching can use allusion and reminiscence, too. But how the word play works depends in part on what the words really are, how they are best translated, and what quotes or recalls what.)

There is another echo here, or a foreshadowing. The Baptist declares that Jesus is the lamb, and the reader who knows Scripture thinks of the Passover lamb. In John's Gospel alone, Jesus is slain on the day the paschal lamb is sacrificed, and so the story of the Crucifixion recalls the story of the Passover. The blood that flows from Jesus' side recalls the blood placed on the doors, redemption recalls redemption, and Calvary echoes exodus *(see John 19:31)*.

Let one more example suffice. This is the word God speaks of Jesus in the story of Jesus' baptism in Matthew 3:17: "This is my Son, the Beloved, with whom I am well pleased." The text recalls at least two Old Testament passages. In Psalm 2:7, God speaks, "I will tell of the decree of the Lord: He said to me, 'You are my son; today I have begotten you.'" Scholars now tell us that this is almost certainly a royal psalm and that the affirmation is God's word of coronation for a king. Does Matthew know this? Does Matthew need to know this? Do we find here both sonship and kingship combined? baptism and coronation? Recognizing the allusion to Psalm 2, we look at its larger context. What does the Lord say to the anointed one next? "Ask of me, and I will make the nations your heritage, and the ends of the earth your possession" (Psalm 2:8). The text points ahead to the next scene in Matthew's Gospel: Satan promises Jesus precisely what the Psalm has promised—power over all the nations of the earth. But Satan's way is the wrong way toward that rule that God promises. The Son must ask the Father, not the tempter, for proper dominion. The right way to such dominion, the whole Gospel will show, is a way of suffering and obedience until at the end—suffering and obedience endured at last—all authority is given to God's anointed one (Matt. 28:16-18).

Isaiah 42:1 picks up the latter part of God's affirmation of Jesus. "Here is my servant, whom I uphold, my chosen, in whom my soul delights." As the Psalm shows forth one who is both son and king, so the combination with Isaiah suggests the anointing of one who is both son and servant. Does Matthew know that this same "servant" is the one who will suffer in Isaiah 53, where there are the so-called "servant songs"? We do not know. Does it matter? Again we look at the larger context. Isaiah 42:1 continues: "I have put my spirit upon him; he will bring forth justice to the nations." Both Psalm 2 and Isaiah 42, in their context, move us far beyond Jesus and John, these two men side by side in the Jordan, to remind us that what happens here counts for all the nations—to the ends of the earth.

And perhaps there is here, too, one more echo of Genesis 22: "Take your son, your only son . . . whom you love." There is the reminder that sonship, kingship, and servanthood find their fulfillment in the cross.

The text foreshadows other texts in Matthew itself, perhaps especially the story of the Transfiguration. Again we hear the heavenly voice: "This is my Son, the Beloved; with him I am well pleased" (Matt. 17:5). But now the affirmation turns to imperative: "Listen to him!" All these claims of the special status of the Son, King and Servant have a point in the lives of believers. The point is: Listen, follow, and obey.

Later in the development of Christian tradition, the writer of 2 Peter echoes Matthew 17 (which echoes Matthew 3). Now the point is not simply to listen, but to listen to the authentic voice of God as found in the Gospels as opposed to the "cleverly devised myths" that entice people away.

> For we did not follow cleverly devised myths when we made known to you the power and coming of our Lord Jesus Christ, but we had been eyewitnesses of his majesty. For he received honor and glory from God the Father when that voice was conveyed to him by the Majestic Glory, saying, "This is my Son, my Beloved, with whom I am well pleased." We ourselves heard this voice come from heaven, while we were with him on the holy mountain. (2 Pet. 1:16-18)

Hays, looking at echo and intertextuality in Paul's Letters, says we must learn from Paul what we could learn from many other biblical writers as well: "We must learn . . . the art of dialectical imitation, bringing Scripture's witness to God's action in the past to bear as a critical principle on the present, and allowing God's present action among us to illumine our understanding of his action in the past."[10]

So, how do we learn from John's Gospel and Matthew's Gospel, and from Paul when we come as interpreters to preach?

We learn that you do not always have to quote Scripture to use Scripture, and certainly do not have to say "Genesis 22:2" in order to echo Genesis 22:2. The lectionary has been a mixed blessing when it has enticed us to bite off more than we, or our congregation, should rightly chew. Some of the worst preaching I've heard (and a tad of the best) comes when preachers try to link four lectionary passages together. The sermon becomes an acrostic: How do we get from this idea to that? Though I know that there is an honorable tradition that invites the congregation to flip through their Bibles to connect this verse on justification in Romans with that verse on justice in Amos, I fear that that strategy, too, overloads and underillumines the mind.

Instead of forcing parishioners to flip from text to text physically or mentally, why not distinguish text from subtext? Distinguish the central source of the sermon from the allusions, images, stories, and reminders that can illumine that central text and enrich the sermon. Why not use a phrase from the day's psalm as part of the sermon on the Gospel, instead of a mini-exegesis stuck right in the center of the parable? ("Christ the Good Shepherd knows his sheep by name and goes with them even in the valley of the shadow of death.") Why not use an image from the parable suited to the exposition of the psalm? ("For you are with me"—like that shepherd who will not let even one sheep wander or rush from his loving care.)

It may be that Christian people are biblically illiterate, but we can build the stories, the images, and the vocabulary that enrich the congregational store. I may not get your echo the first time, but in time I'll remember what the "far country" was, who got waylaid by thieves, and why the Lamb of God was called a lamb, without your needing to discuss paschal practices with me all over again.

We also learn that our best sermon preparation time will not always be spent with guides to the day's lessons that take the Bible apart one text at a time and urge us to linger exclusively on Matthew 3 or Genesis 22. Our best sermon preparation often will be to immerse ourself in Scripture, to read whole books at one sitting, to read the Gospel that is not assigned for this year's sermons, and to read Obadiah the prophet, who does not make it into the lectionary at all. To make Scripture our home so that we are good and illuminating guides to its comforts, oddities, and surprises.

(And we need only add in passing, as Hays makes clear and as Long in his image of witness makes clear, that texts not only illumine other texts, they illumine our experience and our stories. And—as Karl Barth showed when he preached, not when he talked about preaching—our stories and experiences illumine the scripture. The echoing works both ways and preaches both ways.)

You will note that two kinds of echoes, or allusions, have been discussed here. There are those allusions that we are almost certain the biblical text itself intends (Romans 9 recalling Jeremiah 18; and Matthew 3 as a pastiche of Psalm 2, Isaiah 42, and perhaps Genesis 22). There are those allusions that the interpreter discovers or invents (Romans 9 and Job 38). In between are a host of echoes that may or may not be attributable to the presumed intention of the text (John 3 and Genesis 22; Matthew 3 and Genesis 22). There may be a kind of playfulness in discerning or suggesting connections between text and text, and text and image.[11] Just as it is no sin to use imagination in crafting a sermon, it is no sin to use imagination to discover or suggest ways in which one text may play with or play off another. Scripture itself plays such word games all the time.

Expansions and Applications

Sometimes biblical writers expand on the traditions they know in order to make clearer their meaning or to shift their application.

Michael Fishbane's book *Biblical Interpretation in Ancient Israel* shows how we often can find signs of scribal interpretations within the texts of the Hebrew Bible. (Remember that the scribe is my model of the preacher, as in Matthew 13.) For example, both stylistically and thematically, Deuteronomy 33:4 interrupts the Mosaic blessing with an application of the whole story of Sinai to the scribe's community. At the beginning of Deuteronomy 33, Moses is speaking to the people:

> This is the blessing with which Moses, the man of God, blessed the Israelites before his death. He said:

> The LORD came from Sinai,
> and dawned from Seir upon us;
> he shone forth from Mount Paran.
> With him were myriads of holy ones;
> at his right, a host of his own.
> Indeed, O favorite among peoples,
> all his holy ones were in your charge;
> they marched at your heels,
> accepted direction from you. (Deut. 33:1-3)

Then, some early scribe adds a comment that is a third-person application of the text to his own readers. "Moses charged us with the law, as a possession for the assembly of Jacob" (Deut. 33:4). That is an interruption of Moses' first-person blessing.

"Moses charged us with the law, as a possession for the assembly of Jacob." Though there were no parentheses in the Hebrew text, one can hear the verse as a parenthetical addition to an earlier tradition. Later yet, the Septuagint and perhaps, depending on the Septuagint, Ben Sira (24:23) quote this same text and expand its application even further: *the assembly* (or *congregation*) *of Jacob* becomes the *synagogues of Jacob*, affirming Moses as lawgiver not only for the assembly of Israel, but for the emerging synagogues of a later time.[12]

There are interpretive expansions within the text of the New Testament as well. We do not know, for instance, whether the author of Mark began his writing with earlier texts or whether he depended on stories passed on by word-of-mouth, but we can see the work of an interpreter. In the following passage, the NRSV adds the parentheses that the punctuation-free Greek manuscripts would have lacked, but the parentheses seem an appropriate acknowledgment of the fact that a story is expanded by the writer to make the point and perhaps even the application clear:

Now when the Pharisees and some of the scribes who had come from Jerusalem gathered around him, they noticed that some of his disciples were eating with defiled hands, that is, without washing them. (For the Pharisees, and all the Jews, do not eat unless they thoroughly wash their hands, thus observing the tradition of the elders; and they do not eat anything from the market unless they wash it; and there are also many other traditions that they observe, the washing of cups, pots, and bronze kettles.) So the Pharisees and the scribes asked him, "Why do your disciples not live according to the tradition of the elders, but eat with defiled hands?" (Mark 7:1-5)

Here the parenthetical sentences explain to non-Jewish readers the Jewish customs on which the controversy about cleanliness depends.

This is one of those signs that Mark was written for a Gentile Christian audience. Matthew, I believe, used Mark as the major source for his own Gospel, but it also seems likely that the Christians for whom he writes had grown up as Jews and learned the faith that Mark needs to explain. So when Matthew tells this story, he revises by omission, simply leaving out the lengthy explanation of cleanliness customs that his readers or hearers would already know *(cf. Matt. 15:1-2)*.

Sometimes the work of the editor is not as obvious as in these additions and omissions. Sometimes the evangelist simply reshapes a story's nuances in such a way as to make a point appropriate to his audience—a homiletical interpretation. Matthew, I already suggested, may be the archetypical Christian scribe. Certainly he applies tradition he receives, including tradition from Mark, to his own situation. We can look, for instance, at the two different versions of Jesus' controversy about divorce.

Here is Mark's telling of the story:

Some Pharisees came, and to test [Jesus] they asked: "Is it lawful for a man to divorce his wife?" He answered them, "What did Moses command you?" They said, "Moses allowed a man to write a certificate of dismissal and to divorce her." But Jesus said to them, "Because of your hardness of heart he wrote this com-

mandment for you. But from the beginning of creation, 'God
made them male and female.' 'For this reason a man shall leave
his father and mother and be joined to his wife, and the two shall
become one flesh.' So they are no longer two, but one flesh.
Therefore what God has joined together, let no one separate."

Then in the house the disciples asked him again about this
matter. He said to them, "Whoever divorces his wife and marries another commits adultery against her; and if she divorces
her husband and marries another, she commits adultery."
(Mark 10:2-12)

Notice that in this telling of the story the issue is whether
divorce is ever permissible for faithful people. Jesus addresses
the issue in a general way and apparently allows no exceptions to
his rule that people should not divorce, and that if they should
divorce they certainly should not remarry. There is, however,
one place in the story where it looks as though Mark adds something to the tradition he has received. There was no provision
under Jewish law for a wife to divorce a husband, while under
Roman law there was such a provision. Speaking to the circumstances of his audience, Mark probably adds the last part of
verse 12 to the tradition he has received. Again one can almost
imagine the preacherly parentheses: ("and if she divorces her
husband and marries another, she commits adultery").

In Matthew's retelling of the story, the question of the Pharisees is put slightly differently, not "Is it lawful for a man to
divorce his wife?" but "Is it lawful for a man to divorce his wife
for any cause?" (Matt. 19:3). This form of the question probably reflects a debate within the first-century Jewish community
about the interpretation of Deuteronomy 24:1 where Moses
says that the grounds of a certificate of divorce should be what
the Hebrew calls *erwat dabar*, and what the NRSV translates
something objectionable. Some Jewish leaders of the first century thought that phrase ought to be interpreted very broadly:
if a wife did anything to evoke her husband's displeasure (burn
the roast; forget to sweep the house), he could write the cer-

tificate of divorce. Other Jewish leaders thought that *something objectionable* really meant "something shameful" and referred especially to sexual transgressions; on those grounds a man might legitimately divorce his wife. In Matthew, as the Pharisees put the question of divorce to Jesus, that is apparently the question they are asking: what are the legitimate grounds of divorce? And in the somewhat expanded answer that Jesus gives to that question, the Jewish debate is addressed: "And I say to you, whoever divorces his wife, except for unchastity, and marries another commits adultery" (Matt. 19:9). Further, in another interpretive nonexpansion, Matthew omits any reference to a wife divorcing a husband. Clearly he reinterprets the Marcan story for his own audience (an audience perhaps closer to Jesus' original listeners than Mark's audience).

Or look at Matthew's retelling of Mark's passion narrative.

Here is Mark on the passers-by deriding Jesus as Jesus hangs on the cross: "Aha! You who would destroy the temple and build it in three days, save yourself, and come down from the cross" (Mark 15:29-30).

Here is Matthew presenting his version of that harassment: "You who would destroy the temple and build it in three days, save yourself! If you are the Son of God, come down from the cross" (Matt. 27:40). Matthew echoes Mark but also echoes his own Gospel: "If you are the Son of God, command these stones to become loaves of bread. . . . If you are the Son of God, throw yourself down [from the temple]" (Matt. 4:3, 6).

Neither Martin Scorcese nor Nikos Kazantzakis was the first to think of the passion as the last temptation of Christ. The last temptation is the temptation to come down from the cross, give it up, go home. Why does Matthew so expand the story he has? To enrich our understanding of Christ's temptation? To enrich the understanding of first-century Jewish Christians enticed to give up the risk of their fidelity and return to the synagogues from which they came?

We can move from the biblical interpreters to ourselves. Sometimes we are told it is heresy to expand on the biblical stories we preach, to read between the lines. Did my student commit heresy when she preached on the prodigal son's mother? She certainly stretched the text beyond its usual boundaries, but it was *that* text she stretched. Did Matthew stretch Q's *blessed are the poor* into *blessed are the poor in spirit* as an act of impiety, or of piety?

My own sense is that preaching these days is less apt to suffer from a surplus of imagination than from a lack of imagination. I do not know that I want us to sin boldly, but I do want us to preach a little more boldly. We are so scared of allegorizing and psychologizing that we may be afraid of mattering. We get it all right, every exegetical jot and tittle, but what does it matter? Whom does it save? We preach as if we were going to be graded by our seminary Bible professors, not as if we wanted to change the lives of our people. Perhaps by preaching biblically we can do as biblical writers did with the traditions they received. We can use the text as a fountain for our thought and not as a straitjacket.[13]

Typology

Another way in which biblical scribes bring forth from God's storehouse treasures old and new is by the use of typology. At least, as we usually understand it, typology is different from allegory. Allegory uses figures or events as signs for heavenly or eternal realities above human history. Typology takes one figure from history and sees that person as prefiguring another. Typology presupposes two real things and their relationship.

Adam and Christ in Romans 5 are related typologically and, of course, dialectically as well. For Paul, Adam and Christ are very much the same in that their stories encompass the story of all of humankind. They are very different in that one was disobedient, and the other obedient. They are very different in that Christ's obedience undoes Adam's disobedience altogether.

There are sometimes rhetorical clues to help us spot typology: *As . . . so* ("As all die in Adam, so all will be made alive in Christ" [1 Cor. 15:22]); and *If . . . how much more!* ("If, because of the one man's trespass, death exercised dominion, . . . much more surely will those who receive the . . . free gift . . . exercise dominion in life. . . ." [Rom. 5:17]).

Much of the book of Hebrews is a typological comparison and contrast between the Old Testament Joshua and the New Testament Joshua. The first readers of the book of Hebrews read the Scripture in Greek. The name of the first Joshua was translated into Greek, which we translate into English as "Jesus." So for Greek-speaking Christians, both Moses' great successor and God's Son were named Jesus. In rather different ways, both the first Joshua and the second follow and replace Moses. Just as the first Jesus led people into the land Moses promised but did not attain, so the second and greater Jesus is about to lead the faithful into that Canaan, that sabbath, where he has gone before. Like the other Joshua, Jesus is a pioneer, a pioneer and perfecter of our faith. He enters God's rest before us; he brings us there to join him. The rhetorical features are implicit, but they are there. "If Joshua brought the children of Israel into the Promised Land, the new Joshua will bring us into God's rest. If the first sabbath granted peace to God's people, how much more will the new sabbath grant." Typology plays against dialectic; how much the same and how much different are the former promise and the new.

And in the Old Testament, too, the older themes prefigure the later ones. The Second Isaiah reminds a people in exile that they have been brought home before; the first exodus from Egypt prefigures a new exodus from Babylon.

> Thus says the LORD,
>   who makes a way in the sea,
>   a path in the mighty waters,
> who brings out chariot and horse,
>   army and warrior;

> they lie down; they cannot rise;
>> they are extinguished,
>>> quenched like a wick:
> Do not remember the former things,
>> or consider the things of old.
> I am about to do a new thing;
>> now it springs forth, do you not perceive it?
> I will make a way in the wilderness
>> and rivers in the desert. (Isa. 43:16-19)

Note the play between type and antitype, exodus and return from exile. They are alike but not alike. God again leads people forth in mercy, but on the old journey God made a dry place in the midst of the sea. In the new journey God brings forth a river in the midst of the dry land. Exodus and new exodus are alike and not alike; redemption is both repetition and reversal.

Typology can still work powerfully today.

Often African Americans are good guides to typological theology and typological preaching. In black churches, people would sing and hear "Go Down, Moses." Moses and the exodus were not only "over there" and "back then," they were "here and now." Pharaoh and Mrs. Pharaoh looked a lot like the lord and lady of the house. Martin Luther King, Jr., making his last testament, stood on the mountain and looked over into Canaan. He knew he was not Moses, and he knew he was.

Nora Tubbs Tisdale of Princeton Seminary often reminds her students that in preaching we need not be afraid to name God in the world. When we name God in the world, we often will want to do it typologically, to draw the lines between those stories and our stories.

We will not be naive about it: every typology is alike and not alike. First Church is not really First Church of Corinth, and the new and unduly popular associate minister is not really that upstart Apollos, but there are lines and connections that can be made with the help of the Holy Spirit, prayer, imagination, and a little homiletical courage.

Christian faith depends on the assumption that the adage "That was then and this is now" is far too simple. God's "then" impinges on our "now," and our "now" helps us celebrate God's "then."

Correcting and Arguing

Finally, Scripture sometimes corrects Scripture.

Fishbane's book is a treasure trove of intracanonical improvement. For instance, the injunctions of Leviticus 25 about the keeping of sabbath years when Israel shall not till the land or harvest crops: The original text leaves a puzzle. What shall people eat during these seventh years? Leviticus 25:20-22 shows evidence of scribal elaboration and correction:

> Should you ask, What shall we eat in the seventh year, if we may not sow or gather in our crop? I will order my blessing for you in the sixth year, so that it will yield a crop for three years. When you sow in the eighth year, you will be eating from the old crop; until the ninth year, when its produce comes in, you shall eat the old.[14]

Perhaps most enticing is Fishbane's claim that the book of Job attempts an ironic correction of Psalm 8's sanguine view of the human condition. From the perspective of Job's author, the psalmist overestimates both humankind and the divine kindness. Here is Psalm 8:3-6:

> When I look at your heavens, the work of your fingers,
>   the moon and the stars that you have established:
> what are human beings that you are mindful of them,
>   mortals that you care for them?
>
> Yet you have made them a little lower than God,
>   and crowned them with glory and honor.

Here is Job, afflicted:

> What are human beings, that you make so much of them,
>   that you set your mind on them,
> visit them every morning, test them every moment?
> Will you not look away from me for a while,
>   let me alone until I swallow my spittle? (Job 7:17-19) [15]

Or again, suggests Fishbane, look at Isaiah 40:28:

> Have you not known? Have you not heard?
> The LORD is the everlasting God,
>   the Creator of the ends of the earth.
> He does not faint or grow weary;
>   his understanding is unsearchable.

Fishbane suggests that this is a correction of Genesis 2:2, or of a possible misunderstanding of that text: "And on the seventh day God finished the work that he had done, and he rested on the seventh day from all the work that he had done."[16]

In John's Gospel Jesus corrects the same text or its misinterpretation. "Therefore the Jews started persecuting Jesus, because he was doing such things on the sabbath. But Jesus answered them, 'My Father is still working, and I also am working'" (John 5:16-17).

However, John's Gospel is not content to correct a reading, or misreading, of the Old Testament. That Gospel also "corrects" certain claims or motifs of the tradition we find in the Synoptic Gospels.[17]

Here is Mark on Jesus facing his crucifixion: "[Jesus] said, 'Abba, Father, for you all things are possible; remove this cup from me; yet, not what I want, but what you want'" (Mark 14:36). Here is John's correction of that scene: "'Now my soul is troubled,' [says Jesus]. 'And what should I say—"Father, save me from this hour"? No, it is for this reason that I have come to this hour. Father, glorify your name'" (John 12:27-28*a*).

John is not the only New Testament author who corrects or argues with tradition. For instance, in introducing John the Baptist, both Matthew and Luke correct Mark's slightly inaccurate citation of the Old Testament. Mark says "As it is written in the prophet Isaiah . . ." and then proceeds to a citation that conflates Malachi 3:1 with Isaiah 40:3. Both the other synoptic evangelists omit the quotation from Malachi, so that all the words attributed to Isaiah were actually found in the book of Isaiah. While both Matthew and Luke omit the Malachi citation, Luke adds to the tradition he found. Mark and Matthew take from Isaiah 40 only verse 3. "The voice of one crying out in the wilderness, 'Prepare the way of the Lord, make his paths straight.'"[18] Luke, however, goes on to quote Isaiah 40:4-5: " 'Every valley shall be filled, and every mountain and hill shall be made low, and the crooked shall be made straight, and the rough ways made smooth; and all flesh shall see the salvation of God' " (Luke 3:5-6).

These verses expand the significance of the Isaiah quotation for the purposes of Luke's Gospel. Now Scripture foretells the spread of the gospel to the ends of the earth, and the claim that "all flesh shall see God's salvation" points ahead to that other crucial scriptural citation of Acts 2:17: "In the last days it will be, God declares, that I will pour out my Spirit upon all flesh" (*cf. Joel 2:28*). Notice what happens here. Matthew and Luke take Mark as their source; both correct him by providing an accurate citation of Isaiah. Luke "expands" Mark by drawing on the larger context of the Isaiah quotation to find there themes that Mark touched implicitly, if at all.

One way of reading the Epistle of James and its discussion on faith and works is that James seeks to correct Paul, or at least to correct some Paulinists.

> What good is it, my brothers and sisters, if you say you have faith but do not have works? Can faith save you? If a brother or sister is naked and lacks daily food, and one of you says to them,

"Go in peace; keep warm and eat your fill," and yet you do not supply their bodily needs, what is the good of that? So faith by itself, if it has no works, is dead. . . . Was not our ancestor Abraham justified by works when he offered his son Isaac on the altar? You see that faith was active along with his works, and faith was brought to completion by the works. Thus the scripture was fulfilled that says, "Abraham believed God, and it was reckoned to him as righteousness. . . ." (James 2:14-17; 21-23)

This certainly looks to be an argument with Paul's reading of the Abraham story in Romans 4:1-15 and Galatians 3:6-18. (Notice that Genesis 15:6 is interpreted in the light of Genesis 22.) My own reading of Paul's writings suggests that James misreads Paul, or reads only Paul's looser interpreters. Nonetheless, we can understand James' concern. Paul, taken too fervently, can lead to antinomianism. We can understand Matthew correcting Mark; being the good scribe that he is, Matthew knows a wrong citation when he sees one. And we can understand Luke finding in the text Mark cites a context broad enough to include Luke's worldwide vision. We can understand John correcting Mark; if John is encouraging his fellow believers to break from the synagogue, with all the risk that entails, he wants to model steadfastness and not doubt. The new Christians of John's community might not emerge from their own Gethsemane's as bravely as Jesus.[19]

So how do we interpreters honor the tradition of Scripture arguing with Scripture, even correcting it? Certainly not in the ancient style of deciding to keep what we like and toss the rest, and not like the Yale professor who reputedly buttressed some claim this way: "Our Lord has said . . . St. Paul affirms . . . and I am inclined to agree." But the canon itself does give us warrant to have a lover's quarrel with it.

In my youth I had the privilege and danger of serving as a co-resource person with the late Joseph Sittler. Our job was to help preachers deal with difficult texts, and the difficult text assigned for the evening's discussion was the near-sacrifice of

Isaac in Genesis 22. I spent the first half hour discussing ways in which I thought the text could be preached—for all its difficulty. Sittler spent the last half hour suggesting the reasons why the text should not be preached at all.

Over the years I've come more and more to appreciate the wisdom of his approach, but perhaps there is a middle ground. Could we occasionally preach a sermon on why this is not an easy text to preach about? Could I confess, for example, how my mind has changed in the years since Sittler and I held our discussion? My life has changed. When I made my presentation I had no children of my own; now I have two. "Take your son . . . whom you love" has existential bite as it did not in the days of my youth. My Christology has changed. Not that far out of graduate school, I was not only impressed with, I was enamored of some of the claims of substitutionary doctrines of the atonement. God spared us at the expense of his own son. Now I wonder whether a doctrine of the atonement, a doctrine that runs the risk of making God sound like an abusive parent, is congruent with the gospel. My ease with the text is not helped by my dis-ease with instances of child abuse—sometimes religiously driven child abuse—so evident in our society.

What about a sermon on Genesis 22 that raises the questions without jumping to premature answers?

Or what of Ephesians 5? Is there oppressive patriarchy there? Do not pretend it is not there but preach sermons that raise questions. The Bible itself raises questions. We read 1 Corinthians and discover that the Paul who says that "in Christ there is neither male nor female" sometimes says other things that seem contradictory. As preachers, how are we faithful to a Bible that sometimes argues with itself?

Sometimes when we preach "the Bible says," that is the end of the matter. Sometimes it is just the beginning.

The World in Front of the Text

Preachers of my generation who attended so-called mainline seminaries were trained above all in the historical-critical method. We were taught that we could only understand what a text means for contemporary Christians if we first understood what the text meant in its original context—for its original author or its original readers. In the years since I graduated, for a host of reasons, many alternative methods of biblical study have emerged in the seminaries, and especially in colleges and universities. This proliferation of methods in part can be understood by a quick foray into the sociology of knowledge. Why do scholars now learn and teach the methods that they do?

It may be true, as the Preacher says, that there is nothing new under the sun, but every aspiring scholar hopes that the promotion and tenure committee has not discovered that yet. The Bible, after all, is not that big as a collection of literature, and the New Testament is downright tiny. At least students of Victorian literature have Dickens, Thackeray, Trollope, and Eliot, but students of the New Testament have only 284 double-column pages of an NRSV Bible. As religious studies departments in colleges and universities have (blessedly) grown larger, so has the number of people earning their living by writing about the Bible. Each year, many of those in North America who teach the Bible attend the annual meeting of the Society of Biblical Literature. If you divided the New Testament up among the professional scholars enrolled at any such meeting, each scholar would have a very small fraction of a page to claim as his or her specialty. The Dead Sea Scrolls were a godsend for dissertation and article writers, but acts of God, as we all know, cannot be programmed; and it has been a while. The texts we can look at do not multiply, so what can we do? We can multiply our methods.

Fortunately, scholars in literature departments and history departments also need promotion and tenure; so they, too, have multiplied methods. Today we have new criticism (now old), structuralism, deconstruction, poststructuralism, and new historicism for the literary critics. Historians write about social history, statistical history, ethnography, economic history, and so on . . . and on.

That saves biblical critics the trouble of having to invent new methodologies for our task; we can borrow them. We are always a few years, or a few decades, behind the other scholars, but they are not paying much attention; and what we have discovered is new to our guild at least. So we publish and we pray.

For many of us, there is the dim memory that the study of Scripture was once intended to serve the preaching of the church; but however faithful we may be on Sunday, few of us get paid by the church on Monday through Saturday. Even those of us who teach in seminaries, especially seminaries that dwell in the shadow of research universities, are vividly aware of the standards and concerns of those scholars who are our neighbors, friends, and competitors, and we do want to win their approval by what we do.

That is perhaps a somewhat jaundiced view of the way biblical studies is going, at least jaundiced if, like me, you worry about the connections between biblical scholarship and church. But a little skepticism may help us glean from the new methodologies insights and readings that help our preaching, even though for the most part the methodologies were not designed with our preaching in mind.

The late Norman Perrin, meditating on the values of the newly emerging discipline of structural criticism, once opined in my presence that the test of any new method was whether it helped us actually see the text before us in ways that were rich, fruitful, and persuasive. For believers, and perhaps especially for preachers, that to me seems to be still dead right. I already have shared my conviction that faith and preaching emerge from a lively engagement with the text. The question is, What methods and what scholars help enliven that engagement?

Paul Ricoeur, a philosopher who taught in Paris and Chicago, throughout his various writings, has made distinctions that have proved helpful to me (and to many other students of the Bible). One distinction is between the "hermeneutics of recollection of meaning" and the "hermeneutics of suspicion."[1] The classic summary of the two strategies is this: "Hermeneutics seems to me to be animated by this double motivation: willingness to suspect, willingness to listen; vow of rigor, vow of obedience."[2]

Rather than engage in a full-scale hermeneutical evaluation of current methods in biblical criticism (a task for which I am not really equipped), I want to apply to them a hermeneutics of recollection, or at least of sympathy. What is going on in each of these methods as practiced by some of the best practitioners? What clues might the method provide for preaching? If some suspicion creeps in, that will still be in the context of a general appreciation of more recent trends in biblical studies.

The other distinction I borrow from Ricoeur and find helpful as we begin our study of biblical studies is this: when we interpret a text, we will do well to think about the world in front of the text more than the world behind the text.

Ultimately, what I appropriate is a proposed world. The latter is not *behind* the text, as a hidden intention would be, but *in front of* it, as that which the work unfolds, discovers, reveals. Henceforth, to understand is *to understand oneself in front of the text.* It is not a question of imposing on the text our finite capacity of understanding, but of exposing ourselves to the text and receiving from it an enlarged self, which would be the proposed existence corresponding in the most suitable way to the world proposed.[3]

To put it in other terms, Ricoeur suggests that we should pay more attention to the narrative world the story creates than, say, the Palestinian world in which the story was created. Many New Testament interpreters think Ricoeur has that just right; others still read texts archaeologically to dig out where they came from, and others think that both strategies pretend to give the text more autonomy than it can claim.

I want to use Ricoeur's distinction to point out three major movements within biblical criticism. Some critics worry about the world in front of the text, some worry about the world behind the text, and some worry about the world we bring to the text.

Literary Criticism of the Bible

Biblical critics who also call themselves literary critics are concerned to help us discover the world in front of the text, the world the text projects.

The oldest form of such literary criticism still alive is the so-called "new criticism." Like the "young adult" class at church which moved through middle age toward senescence, new criticism has been with us since the midcentury, when its most noted practitioners taught at Yale.

New criticism dealt primarily with poetry and made two claims that had obvious implications for biblical study as well.

The first claim was that much earlier criticism had practiced the "intentional fallacy," seeking to discover what the poet meant by the poem he or she wrote. According to these critics, it does not matter what the poet intended; what matters is what the poem does—the world in front of the text, not the world behind it. In order to interpret poetry, we do not ask the poet, we ask the poem.[4]

Closely related was the claim that critics ought not commit the heresy of paraphrase (the theological language is not altogether coincidental).[5] The heresy was the notion that the poem could be paraphrased. "I have promises to keep / and miles to go before I sleep" writes Robert Frost as the last line of his poem "Stopping by Woods on a Snowy Evening."[6]

"Let me paraphrase," says the heretical reader: "The poet or the protagonist has a bunch of errands to do over a fairly wide terrain, and the day is getting a little shorter. Perhaps he or she is also a little tired."

"No, no," says another heretical reader. "The poet or the protagonist looks at the obligations that come with life—their number and their duration—and looks toward death as both the conclusion and the terminus of that journey. Does death mark a goal toward which the poet goes with some relief? Or is death an interruption which he dreads?"

The "new critics" would say that neither paraphrase will do, partly because they both have a part of it right; but you could multiply paraphrases endlessly and still not have it all. The poem is what the poet does. The story has it that Auden read a poem at a poetry reading to a group of students. "What does your poem mean?" one student asked. The poet read the poem again.

Of course the new critics had many things to say about poems. They wrote comments on versification, structure, meter, metaphor, and borrowings from other poetry. What they avoided was paraphrase, saying what the poem means.

Understandably, the first New Testament critics excited about "new criticism" were students of the parables, which, like poems, are relatively self-contained and full of metaphor.[7]

I came to seminary fresh from a college education in which

I was steeped in the "new criticism." In our seminary courses on the parables, however, we were influenced not by Wimsatt or Brooks, but by Joachim Jeremias and C. H. Dodd. Both of these scholars wrote careful books insisting that each parable had one and only one point, and that the purpose of interpretation was to get that point right. Getting the point right meant two things: (1) being able to paraphrase the parable's point, and (2) showing that that point reflected the intentionality of Jesus (or, in some cases, of the evangelist).[8] Eight blocks down the street from the divinity school classroom, Wimsatt and Brooks were teaching away, but in the early sixties we budding preachers had not yet attended to their point.

Not long after, the new critics of the parables began to make their claims. Here is what the parable meant and therefore what it means, said those older scholars. No, said the younger turks. "Ask what the parable does. Don't assume there's only one point, and for heaven's sake don't paraphrase that point. Don't interrogate Jesus or St. Luke; interrogate the text."[9]

I must confess that the "new criticism" of parables helped my preaching perhaps more clearly and concretely than any other methodological move this study will trace. I started letting stories be stories and metaphors be metaphors. Jesus no longer told parables in order to illustrate what he very well could have put into other words, making the New Testament even shorter than it already is. The story did not have a point; the story was a point. My preaching improved and so did that of countless others.

Take the parable of the good Samaritan and try not to paraphrase it but to see what world it creates (Luke 10:30-37). Notice that it is a story within a story within a story. The story of the good Samaritan is told within the story of the good lawyer which is told within the story of the good man from Nazareth who himself will be waylaid and abandoned.

In the middle story, the narrative frame, it is not surprising that the lawyer is worried about the law, about getting it right, making his case. When he asks "Who is my neighbor?" is he trying to understand his obligation or to get out of it? Who are the people in his neighborhood? Are some of them, God help us, people that he does not meet each day?

Notice how in Jesus' story the lawyer's question gets shifted in two ways. Jesus never does say who counts as the lawyer's neighbor; he shows us who it is who acts neighborly. Or, from a slightly different angle, he does not encourage the lawyer to get his categories right, but to get his actions right. Jesus picks up the first question ("What must I do?") at the expense of the second question ("Who is my neighbor?"). What must I *do*? "*Do* this and you will live." "Go and *do* likewise."

Look at the central story itself. If you just diagram the sentences like the diagrams we had to do in seventh-grade English class, notice how the story plays on the page. Notice the simplicity of apathy and the complexity of compassion. You can pass by the wounded in a couple of words, but to care takes detours, return visits, business transactions, and hands-on medical care.

Who are you in this parable? Are you the one who "does likewise," or are you the one who gets done unto—first robbed and then redeemed by, God help us, the one person in all the world you never dreamed could be your neighbor?

Do not tell us what the passage says, say the new critics, show us what the passage does. It makes a world in front of the text. When you preach, go and do likewise.

Closely related to the new criticism is narrative criticism. As new criticism works most effectively with parable and psalm, narrative criticism works with (obviously) narratives, usually with larger structures; thus the narrative readings of each of the four Gospels, or of the story of David, or of the Joseph saga.[10]

The principles involved are fairly simple. There are several questions any narrative text raises:

1. What is the plot of the story? Narratives have plots. Often what drives plots is conflict.[11] What conflicts are there in your Gospel or your saga? How do they move toward resolution? The conflict between Jacob and his twin brother Esau drives much of the Jacob story. The conflict between Joseph and his brothers drives the early chapters of that narrative. In each case the conflict pushes toward resolution. Jacob and Esau are reunited, if not reconciled; Joseph forgives the brothers who have wronged him. The conflict between the first brothers, Abel and Cain, does not end so happily. The resolution, if there is a resolution, depends on God's query of Cain and God's protection of Cain.

2. Who are the characters in this story? Every narrative has characters. Here, narrative critics all seem to have read E. M. Forster, who distinguishes between round characters (like many of those in Jane Austen's novels) and flat characters (like most of those in Dickens' novels).[12] The former are full of lights and shadows, quirkiness and quiddity. "The test of a round character is whether it is capable of surprising in a convincing way."[13] The latter are one-pony shows; some single trait marks them off. " 'I will never desert Mr. Micawber.' There is Mrs. Micawber—she says she will not desert Mr. Micawber, she does not, and there she is."[14] The truth is, I do not think the categories "round" and "flat" work very well for the Bible. They psychologize the tough fact that often in the Gospels the only fully rounded character is the one we never see—God. In the narratives of the Synoptics, Peter verges on "roundness," and in Acts both Peter and Paul develop from their mistaken views of what God has done and is doing in Jesus Christ to a view more generous and redemptive. Jacob learns new tricks as he goes along, but does he ever stop being a trickster? Perhaps there is development enough in the move from the trickster who dances to the trickster who limps. Judas is the classic flat character. Notice how every time he is introduced we are reminded that he is the betrayer. Jack Miles has written a book that takes the whole Old Testament as its narrative (in the order found in the Hebrew Bible) and argues that the main character of that narrative—God—is rounded, diverse, surprising, and developing.[15]

3. What kind of narrator tells the story? First person? Third person? Omniscient? Limited? More recent novels often have first-person narrations; for example, David Copperfield tells his story, and Holden Caulfield tells his. The narrators do not know everything that is going on; part of the fun of reading is to watch them discover what we readers have already guessed. The Sherlock Holmes stories are third-person narratives whose narrator is not omniscient, Dr. Watson. Biblical narratives have almost always third-person, omniscient narrators. The narrators often not only know what is going on in the minds and intentions of the protagonists, but they often know what is going on in the mind and intention of God. The only exceptions I can think of are those portions of Acts where the narrator seems to be a participant in the action. ("When it was decided that we were to sail for Italy, they transferred Paul and some other prisoners to a centurion of the Augustan Cohort, named Julius" [Acts 27:1].) And there are those brief narrative portions of the Epistles where Paul talks about his own experiences in narrative form *(for instance, look at 2 Cor. 11:21–12:10; Gal. 1:11–2:14)*.[16]

4. How does the narrative use time? Every narrative deals with time. It marches straight ahead, or looks back from the end, or circles around. The way time works shapes the way narratives work. In Mark's Gospel, the story seems to be marching straight along when suddenly we circle back to learn about the circumstances of John the Baptist's execution (Mark 6:17-29). In Exodus, the narrator shows us two sets of events taking place simultaneously. Just when we think Moses' time on the mountain is over and the story is going to move on, time circles back to show us what Aaron and the Israelites were doing while Moses was talking with God *(see Ex. 32:1)*.

5. How is the biblical narrative unified? There is another principle at least implicit in most narrative criticism.

The principle (which does fit with the older "new criticism") is that the classic narratives of the Bible represent an aesthetic unity. Everything fits or can be made to fit. The delight of earlier redaction and form critics in finding what did not fit, where the seams were, and where the traces of older tradition could be found is not adopted by narrative critics. They discern or devise a unity for the story of Jacob whether or not the present narrative represents a long period of development and draws upon several earlier sources. They show how the plot of John's Gospel develops from chapter 1 through chapter 21 without worrying much about whether the prologue of chapter 1 was originally an independent poem, or whether the scenes by the sea in chapter 21 are a late, editorial addition to the "real" Gospel.[17]

Look at Mark's Gospel as narrative:

Conflict: The most obvious conflict in the Gospel of Mark is that between Jesus (and his disciples) and the scribes and Pharisees. The whole section of the Gospel from 2:1 to 3:6 is an embodiment of this conflict. But the conflict is also more complicated than that. On the one hand, Jesus fights not only flesh-and-blood opponents, but principalities and powers—demons and evil spirits. When the Pharisees criticize Jesus' exorcisms, are they not lining themselves up with the forces of Satan against the forces of God? On the other hand, the "loyal" disciples often turn into opponents, not through malice but through stupidity. When Jesus accuses Peter of being Satan, he not only says that this most visible disciple tempts him, he suggests that, like the scribes and Pharisees, Peter has lined up on the wrong side of the great conflict between God's spirit and the spirit of the destroyer. And how does Pilate fit the story? Caught in the middle, does he also become complicit with the enemy (15:15)?[18]

Characters in the Gospel of Mark: Jesus is the central character. Does he develop at all? When the Syrophoenician woman tells Jesus he should be more kind to puppies and to foreign women, does he learn something (7:24-30)? When Jesus asks "Who do you say that I am?" is it a quiz or a quest (8:27)? The disciples in this Gospel seem to develop downhill, starting out hopeful and moving farther and farther away from their own vocation. And the so-called flat characters—seldom named and quickly gone, the anonymous people—actually "get" the Gospel. Maybe in some slight way they remind us of the anonymous author who also gets the Gospel and then writes it down.

The narrator in the Gospel of Mark: The story is narrated in the third person; and the narrator seems to know it all, not only what is going on, but what is going on in the hearts of his characters. Jesus is filled with pity (1:41). His opponents, who appear only to be curious, are actually testing him and out to get him (8:11; 10:2).

The narrator knows the meaning of the story before the story begins; so at the beginning he announces that this is "the beginning of the good news of Jesus Christ, the Son of God" (1:1). The narrator seems even to know the mind of God, inviting God to confirm what the narrator has already told us: "You are my Son, the Beloved" (1:11); and "This is my Son, the Beloved" (9:7).

Furthermore, the narrator knows irony, setting up the story in such a way as to underline its ironic twists. "He saved others; he cannot save himself. Let the Messiah, the King of Israel, come down from the cross now, so that we may see and believe" (15:31-32). The chief priests and scribes think they mock Jesus, but they mock themselves. They speak in jest what is in fact a Christological claim: precisely because he does not save himself he can save others; precisely because he does not come down from the cross the faithful can believe. The narrator lets his narration do his work for him; show, do not tell.

Time in the Gospel of Mark: It is well known that the end is not the end. In Greek, the Gospel ends with silence and a conjunction, "because. . ." (16:8). The beginning may not be what it looks like, either. The first verse says, "The beginning of the gospel of Jesus, Messiah, Son of God" (1:1). Several have suggested that the title of the whole book may be just that: "the beginning of the gospel. . . ." Sixteen chapters and eight verses about the beginning of the good news. If so, then the good news continues beyond the silence and the conjunction in the lives of those who have heard the good news of Jesus, the Messiah, the Son of God.

In discussions on Old Testament narratives, Robert Alter looks at another set of narrative issues: the relationship between narrative structure and apparent digressions. He observes that the story of Sodom in Genesis 18–20 apparently interrupts the usual sequence of an annunciation narrative.[19] Usually in the Old Testament, an annunciation narrative presents the problem of barrenness, the announcement of a promise that the barren woman will bear a child, and the description of the fulfillment of the promise.[20]

Here, Alter reminds us, the narratives of the destruction of Sodom, the incestuous relationship between Lot and his daughters, and the ruse by which Abraham passes off Sarah as his sister to Abimelech all intervene. Each of these stories, Alter suggests, in a different way reminds the reader of the cost of covenant: the promise to Abraham is not unconditional, as we see first in Genesis 18:19, but it depends on righteousness. God says of Abraham: "For I have singled him out so that he might instruct his sons and his family after him, that they should keep the way of the Lord *to do righteousness and justice*" (Gen. 18:19, as translated by Alter).[21]

In Genesis 18–20 we see the ways in which righteousness can be thwarted or evaded, and the dire consequences of that violation. Sodomites threaten gang rape while Lot offers them his virgin daughters. The virgin daughters lose their virginity by intercourse with their drunken father. Abimelech almost falls into injustice, but is spared by his uprightness and the providence of God. Alter summarizes the function of this long interruption:

Propagation appears at the beginning of Genesis as a divinely ordained imperative for humanity. But as the moral plot of human history rapidly thickens into the most terrible twists of violence and perversion, it becomes progressively clear that propagation and survival are precarious matters, conditional, in the view of the Hebrew writers, on moral behavior. . . . Unusual shadows must be cast over the way to fulfillment. The first of these is biological: the extreme old age of the patriarch and, especially of the matriarch. . . . Beyond that, the three intervening episodes of the destruction of Sodom, the act of incest between Lot and his daughters, and the sojourn in Gerar convey to us an urgent new sense of perilous history which is the thematically needed prelude to the birth of Abraham's son. . . . The historical scene Isaac is about to enter is indeed a checkered one, and he and his offspring will have troubles enough of their own, in regard to both moral performance and physical survival.[22]

Furthermore, Alter suggests, the whole narrative of the Hebrew Bible from Genesis through 2 Kings provides, if not a structure, at least a tapestry, with themes (including that of the promise to Abraham, and the horrible example of Sodom) repeated, refigured throughout. It is not a neat story perhaps, but a story shaped into patterns and promises.[23]

What might we learn from narrative criticism about preaching? The stress on longer narratives might wean us from our fixation with the pericope. Lectionary or no, it is almost impossible to preach on a few verses from the book of Jonah, Genesis 17, or the book of Job without attending to the entire narrative. Perhaps we should sometimes preach with the same sense of the whole structure of Mark, John, or even Luke-Acts. Of course we still will preach selectively, but our selections might illumine the whole larger narrative.

Certainly as we prepare sermons we will want to set pericopes within the larger narrative frameworks where they sometimes belong. Even with Paul's Epistles, our sermons are often helped if we can place Paul's words about freedom from the law (in Galatians) within narrative frameworks—the framework of his argument with the Galatian Christians, or the framework of his argument with Peter.

We will sometimes ask of those larger narratives the kinds of questions the narrative critics suggest. "Not just *how* does this story work?" but "How does this story forward the plot? What conflict is involved here? How might it be resolved? What kind of character is this?"

Sometimes we will preach sermons that are themselves narrative. When we do, we will learn from the narrative critics that sometimes the gospel is best preached by indirection, but we also will note that (unlike many contemporary short stories, for example) the Gospel writers often give fairly clear and vivid clues to what they think their story means. Occasional puzzlement on the part of our congregations may be a gift; constant befuddlement probably violates their legitimate expectations of us as preachers.

We will look for other narratives to help illumine the central narratives of the biblical text, but those other narratives will be used to illumine, not to replace, the foundational stories. Our congregations rightly will be more interested to hear the story of Paul's call time after time than they will to hear (once again!) about our own.

Early in my ministry I preached many sermons that were shaped entirely as story. Now I preach few and am more inclined to use story as one part of a larger and, in some ways, more complicated mix. Writing a good story (or even a pretty good story) is hard work, but I do not think it is just because I am getting lazy that I have diminished the number of times I use that mode of preaching.

For one thing, I have discovered that some members of every congregation find stories confusing rather than helpful. They just do not think narratively; and if they live narratively, they do not know it. The sermon does not seem the right time to revise their epistemology. Some people get narratives; some people get propositions. Both kinds of people are listening to us preach.

Furthermore, I have discovered that my congregation wants to know what I believe. The way I tell the story tells a lot about what I believe, but it does so indirectly. We used to be very afraid of authoritarianism, but sometimes I think we avoided authoritarianism by avoiding clarity. Of course God is a mystery, but I have a particular take on that mystery, and people sometimes want me to express that as clearly and simply as I can. Stories help that telling but do not entirely compose it.

And I am getting older. Indirection seemed more appropriate when I had lots of time. Now that I have less, I am more apt to do my own modest version of "Here I stand. God help me; I can do no other."

If new criticism and narrative criticism look at the world in front of the text, then reader-response criticism looks at the world between the text and reader, but with special emphasis on the reader. In fact, as reader-response criticism is practiced by Robert Fowler on the Gospel of Mark, the test of a reading is not the intention of the writer or intent of the text, but of what the reader finds there.

> [Traditional] perspectives assume that meaning is available in or through the text, independent of the reader. What if we take seriously the role of the reader in determining the meaning of the text? Regardless of whether the text is considered a window or a mirror, does it matter who is doing the looking? What if, instead of considering meaning as something static, unchanging, and preceding the reading experience, we consider it a dynamic, ever-changing creation of the reader in the act of reading.[24]

As one reads reader-response criticism, it is clear that the best critics understand interpretation as an event taking place over time; one reads Mark 13 remembering what one has read in Mark 4. One brings to the reading both one's own experience and the memories and impressions derived from what he or she already has read in the text.

As I read reader-response critics, it is not always clear what reader the critic has in mind. Sometimes the reader response seems to trace the putative responses of an early "original" reader of the text. What did a first-century Christian hear or see in Mark's Gospel while reading it for the first time? Sometimes the reader imagined is a kind of ideal present reader, one who brings to bear critical questions and issues appropriate to the late twentieth century. Less often is there attention to a "real" reader, a reader who would bring to the text not only an open mind and a literary imagination, but a set of biases, questions, theological or anti-theological presuppositions, and the hangover from a bad day at the office.[25]

A classic example of reader-response interpretation is from Fowler's dissertation and is richly expanded in his full study of Mark, *Let the Reader Understand.* How does the wise reader respond to the two feeding narratives in Mark's Gospel? The wise reader is astonished to discover that at the second narrative the disciples are just as befuddled as they were at the first. Two chapters and maybe two days after Jesus has fed five thousand hungry people, he finds himself with four thousand other hungry people. The disciples ask, "How can one feed these people with bread here in the wilderness" (Mark 8:4)? The wise reader may understand echoes of manna and Exodus and will certainly understand that the disciples are not wise at all. They are dense.[26]

Look at another example from the Gospels: a reader-response reading of Matthew 25. Usually when we study or preach we preach one of these three stories at a time; but look at how they work when we hear them in order.

The chapter begins with Jesus telling a story. What is the kingdom like, or our response to it? We get the story of ten maidens, five wise and five foolish. In the time of crisis the foolish want to borrow oil from the wise, but in matters of the kingdom you are responsible for yourself and you need to take care of the gifts you've been given. The specific gifts are not specified in the narrative, but if we have been reading or listening to Matthew's Gospel, we can suspect that they include faith and obedience. In the light of the parable, and awaiting God's impending realm, the reader's response is, "Oh, I'd better be careful."

But not *too* careful; so Jesus tells a second story. What is the kingdom like, or our response to it? Now the kingdom is like the story of the talents, and faithfulness is not just caution, but creativity—to act out our lives in the image of God. The poor one-talent servant has caught the master's nature truly but ironically: "Master, I knew that you were a harsh man, reaping where you did not sow, and gathering where you did not scatter seed" (25:24). The parable tells the listener: "Go and do likewise. Make much of little, spend your gifts." The listener or reader responds: "I'm on my way; throw caution to the winds." Prodigal fidelity. But note that fidelity has a particular shape.

What *is* the kingdom? Jesus has said the kingdom of God is like the maidens and is like the servants, but now in this chapter there are no more parables. Now Jesus reveals how it will be when the Son of Man comes in his glory. This is not a chapter of three parables, but of two parables and a flat-out description. The description does use a simile, that of sheep and goats, and the description makes this fundamental claim: how the readers or listeners serve the least of Christ's brethren is how they serve Christ. Now it is clear that both fidelity and creativity are used in the service of charity and justice, but we do not get to that insight without thinking through responsibility and creativity (the maidens and the talents) first.

How does reader-response criticism help in our preaching?

As my reading of Matthew 25 or Fowler's reading of the entire Gospel of Mark indicates, reader-response interpretations often work best with larger units or even whole Gospels. Because the method is temporal and dynamic, it requires development—shifts, nuances, echoes, repetitions. It may be hard to cover enough of the temporal experience of reading in the limited time for the Sunday sermon, especially for lectionary preaching, which can chop up our material. If we can count on people coming to hear us week after week and remembering this week some of what they heard last week, we can perhaps help them hear the development of the Gospel or the narrative, not just this week's particular story.

Certainly we as preachers will want to understand how a particular passage fits in the whole reading, or hearing, of the Gospel of Mark. We may not want to summarize the whole Gospel every time we come to the story of James and John requesting seats on the right and left of Jesus in glory, the passage where Jesus asks if they can be baptized with his baptism and drink his cup (Mark 10:35-40). We as readers/hearers, however, will remember the story of Jesus' own baptism and will think ahead to the cup at the upper room and the cup at Gethsemane. We will remember that the next time we see someone at Jesus' right hand and at his left that they will not be James and John, but the two thieves. Moreover, reader-response criticism may be a rich resource for preachers as we attend to listener-response preaching. The most effective preachers always imagine those in the pew and try to "hear" what is being said from the pulpit, a feat of imagination or grace which often marks the difference between being only correct and being both correct and persuasive.[27] Books like Fowler's help us hear the text and think about how people hear our interpretations of that text.

Perhaps I should add also that, in my experience, congregations almost never are made of "ideal" listeners—the ones who come with the questions we wish they had or with the openness we wish they shared. Part of good preaching is to be aware of those resistances in members of the congregation—the places where what we say is very hard to hear. Sometimes that means we will try to say it differently; sometimes that means we will keep saying it in the hope that the Holy Spirit will work nonetheless.

One of Fowler's old friends now has deserted him academically, though I hope not personally. Stephen Moore, who writes about deconstruction and post-structuralism, has drunk deeply of Derrida and Foucault, trying to show us what we may learn from their iconoclastic reading of the texts.

To caricature, if new critics look at the text, and reader-response critics look at the interaction between text and reader, then Moore and the critics he seeks to recruit look at the text as occasion for a brand-new text—the interpretation. Every criticism is itself a new work of art, with authority equal to the authority of the text it interprets.

So, Moore and Janice Capel Anderson write:

> Deconstruction is suspicious of the power often attributed to authors to bend the language of texts to their will to use language only and not be used by it. For deconstruction, language is an extremely slippery, infinitely resourceful element that refuses to limit itself to what its users intend to say. There is always an unpredictable and uncontrollable excess of meaning that simmers within every text, always ready to spill over. . . inventive or it is nothing at all. As deconstructionists in particular see it, criticism is not qualitatively different from literature. . . . Criticism becomes an unconscious reenactment of the text it sets out to master.[28]

I will start with a problem or paradox and then go briefly to an example of Moore at work. The problem or paradox is this: If a text is open to infinite possibilities of interpretation and the meaning lies not in the text but in what I do with it, then when I interpret Moore, that is not a guide to anything outside my interpretation, just as Moore's interpretation of John's Gospel, say, is not a guide to anything outside his interpretation. And when you interpret me—well, good luck.[29]

I began all of this by stating Norman Perrin's test of any

method: Does a reading open a text to us in a new way? I am forced to confess that in Moore's latest book, *Poststructuralism and the New Testament,* Moore opens up the conversation between Jesus and the Samaritan woman at the well in a new way. He plays off the thirst Jesus confesses at the well with the thirst Jesus confesses on the cross. Maybe Jesus' thirst at the well is not just the rhetorical occasion to instruct the woman about living water; maybe his thirst at the well is his thirst for someone willing to be instructed. From her, too, water pours forth to quench his need to be needed. Jesus makes it sound as though living water is all a matter of spirit; no need to tie it to real wells at all. But, of course, he himself is word made flesh, the paradox that undoes the distinction he tries to make between what is spirit and what is flesh. At the end, before he gives up the Spirit, he cries out for "material water" ("I thirst"). The Samaritan woman's confusion of the spiritual and the material may be more true than Jesus' distinction between them.

> In the process, that other hierarchical structure within which Jesus and the Samaritan woman conversed also has suffered some water damage. I refer, of course, to the hierarchy of male over female. If what Jesus has said to the Samaritan woman is indeed contradicted by what he is, and if what Jesus is has indeed been affirmed by what she has said, then the female student has outstripped her male teacher, even though he himself was the subject of the seminar. She has insisted, in effect, that earthly and heavenly, flesh and Spirit, figurative and literal, are symbiotically related categories: each drinks endlessly of the other, and so each is endlessly contaminated by the other. To draw a clear line between them, as Jesus attempts to do, is about as effective as drawing a line on water.[30]

How odd this is. How puzzling. It makes me want to read it again. Not often in digging through commentaries do I want to read a reading again. Of course, in a footnote Moore says that although he presented his reading this way this time, he could do it just the opposite way next time, and that it would work just as well.[31]

There is much mystery here. Does the mystery move us toward illumination? I am not yet sure.

What I am more sure of is that it is very hard to preach "deconstructively." In part that is because, as I said from the start, preaching grants a certain prior authority to the text that seems very far from some of the postmodern strategies. It is partly because preaching is not a matter of opening up the whole range of possibilities to each individual interpreter. Preaching is a communal event and presupposes a community of hearers. Even if I catch a different nuance in a text or sermon than you do, the preacher hopes that we will have enough commonality that he or she can speak to us both at the same time. More than that, the preacher preaches precisely to build a community of interpretation, interpreters whose community in part grows out of the shared enterprise of hearing the text and the sermon together. As I read deconstruction, it seems both too liberated from the text and too liberated from the community to give us the help we need. But from time to time I find in a poststructuralist reading a new angle that reflects light not just on the interpreter, but on the text.

We are aware of one more movement in literary criticism. The code word for it is "new historicism," though some of its founders are now looking for other words to label it, if indeed there is a "thing" there to label. The new historicism is an attempt to move away from all kinds of criticism that seem unduly formalist, restricted to asking what is going on in a text without asking what is going on in the world out of which the text emerges. It is sometimes hard to find ways to distinguish new historicism from old historical critical studies, but perhaps it helps to say that the older studies tended to talk about the "background" for a Victorian, Renaissance, or biblical text. The new historicism does not make distinctions between background and foreground but tries to describe a kind of complex interweaving of culture and text, where apparently disparate details in the society or the poem help us reflect on the "world" of which the poem is a part. So, A. K. M. Adam writes: "New historicists also resist the "text/context" binary opposition. Texts are part of their context, and the historical context is woven into the text, so that any text may be as much an act of subversive resistance to the prevalent ideas of the time as it is a sign of the times."[32]

There are these premises involved in the movement:

1. Texts are not simply the products of individual creative authors, but reflect the social worlds in which they are written. Authors do not speak simply for themselves, but for and out of a complex and interlayered world.

2. Texts both reflect the worlds from which they arise, and affect those worlds.

3. Sometimes what seem to be the most disparate and unrelated signs of life in the world from where the text emerged (say, Elizabethan England) may provide clues to the deeper structures of that society. They may provide both analogies to the text and evidence for the world that produced it. For Stephen Greenblatt, *The Ambassadors*, a portrait by Holbein, illumines the thoughts and writings of Thomas More, who was a courtier as well as a saint. A sermon by Hugh Latimer illumines the structures of mercy and authority in *Measure for Measure* and *The Tempest*.[33] Often these clues are presented in anecdotal fashion. (Greenblatt also can draw his analogies and anecdotes from quite disparate social settings. The child-rearing practices of Francis Wayland, the American Baptist minister of the Jacksonian era and president of Brown University, provides clues in a reading of *King Lear*.)[34]

4. Literature does not exist in a value-free vacuum. Societies value literature because they get something of value in exchange; literature depends on a society that is willing to sustain it.[35]

5. Although as with poststructuralism the new historicists

often see a variety of "meanings" implicit in any given work of art, they also believe that both text and context provide limits to the range of meanings.

6. For the new historicists (at least for Greenblatt), the *study* of literature and its history is also not value-free. We learn from the study of literature and its history both what our forebears valued and what might, by analogy or contrast, prove valuable for us.

7. Some new historicists are willing to use the personal anecdote to illumine the critical reading. This strategy is particularly evident in the works of Greenblatt and D. A. Miller. Perhaps this is a way of acknowledging the historicity of the critic; he too is embedded in structures beyond his making. Perhaps it is a way of reminding us that history still touches us; we read ourselves in its light, and it in our own.[36]

So far as I know, no biblical scholar has yet declared herself or himself a "new historicist," but there are a few who seem to be moving in that direction.[37]

Dale Martin, who in many ways is the heir of social scientific studies of the Bible, seems also to slant toward some of the insights of the new historicists. His introduction to his book on the metaphor of slavery in early Christian discourse even includes the telling anecdote:

> A fascinating inscription survives from Donysopolis . . . and probably comes from the second or third century C.E. . . . The inscription was erected by a man who seems to have been a slave steward, or manager, of a free man's property. Only four letters of the man's name, "Neik," survive in the fragmentary Greek inscription. "Neik" first confesses to the God a few minor sins. . . . Then Neik concentrates on his major offense: he had apparently promised freedom to one of the family slaves and had registered the slave with the temple as the promissory step toward the slave's manumission. His lord . . . , however, who seems initially not to have known about the agreement, later demanded the certificate of manumission in order to invalidate it.[38]

And the whole book does just what the new historicists seek to do; it shows the intricate interweaving between a text (2 Corinthians 9) and a context: the Greco-Roman world of the first century of our era. Notice indeed the panoply of sources and resources Martin brings to bear on his subject, a list that would warm the heart of a new historicist critic. "In this chapter I use a wide variety of materials—inscriptions, Greco-Roman novels, histories, satires, speeches, and handbooks on household management, agriculture, and dream interpretation—to paint a picture of slavery in the early Roman Empire."[39]

In his book on the metaphor of "slavery" in early Christian discourse, he raises questions that Greenblatt would recognize:

> My subject is the narrowly defined area of one particular function of slavery as a metaphor in early Christianity: how do we explain the positive, soteriological use of slavery as a symbol for the Christian's relationship to God or Christ? If the institution of slavery was as oppressive as it seems to have been, and if Greeks and Romans so feared slavery and despised slaves, how could slavery portray salvation positively for early Christians? Why, in other words, would any person of that society want to be called a slave of Christ? To address these questions in this book I detail the complexity of slavery, and the ambiguity of slave status in Greco-Roman society in order to analyze the religious and social—indeed, ideological—function of slavery as a metaphor in early Christianity, especially in the Pauline church at Corinth.
>
> I had hoped that the shortcomings of a book with such a narrow focus—one function of a metaphor as seen primarily in one text—will be compensated by the offering of a full social and rhetorical placement of the metaphor. Religious language is inextricably intertwined with social structures, ideological constructs, and rhetorical strategies of the society at large.[40]

Again, we can read Martin sounding a good deal like Greenblatt: "When I say an analysis of *slave of Christ* must be contextual, I mean to suggest that that context must be a social one. Too often biblical commentators limit themselves to a world of ideas. . . . To explain language, to understand how metaphors function within a society, we must look to all of a society and everyday experience within it."[41]

Let me draw on one of Martin's interpretations to illustrate how his method illumines texts we thought we understood but may have "understood" only by wrenching them from their historical and social context. The text is 1 Corinthians 7:21-24:

> Were you a slave when called? Do not be concerned about it. Even if you can gain your freedom, make use of your present condition now more than ever. For whoever was called in the Lord as a slave is a freed person belonging to the Lord, just as whoever was free when called is a slave of Christ. You were bought with a price; do not become slaves of human masters. In whatever condition you were called, brothers and sisters, there remain with God.

What is at stake in this passage, suggests Martin, is not whether Christians are free from all patronage; the question is, who is their patron? In the context of that time it was often seen as highly desirable for a slave to move from a relationship to a master of lower status into a relationship to one of higher status and authority. For Christians who have been slaves, their salvation consists in part that they now belong not just to their former masters, but to Christ. Inscriptions and literature of the time indicate that former slaves ("freed persons") still were defined by their position in the economy of a household—whether that of their former owner or that of a new patron. In this passage, Christians who are slaves are assured that their real status consists in their place in Christ's household, where they are freed persons. Their status improves within the household; the household where they work is a great improvement.

On the other hand, because stronger Christians who are themselves patrons or have authority in a household will not

think of themselves as "slaves," Paul insists on a kind of eschatological reversal. In the household of Christ, those who think
of themselves as free people now stand under the authority
and ownership of their true patron.[42]

> Appropriately, therefore, Paul picks out precisely the high-
> status Christian (not even the freed person, but the free man)
> and makes him the slave of Christ, while the slave is elevated
> to a higher position as freed person of Christ. Paul thereby
> redefines the hierarchy of status in the church by employing
> the existing soteriological motif of the Christian as slave of
> Christ and the readily recognized status implications of the
> master-slave and patron-client social structure.[43]

(The issue is somewhat further complicated by the fact that
to be a "slave of Christ" is not necessarily to be without authority; it may be that the slave is a representative, a majordomo for
the master. Paul himself is a "slave of Christ" *(see Rom. 1:1;
Phil. 1:1)*; and this slavery does not conflict with his apostle-
ship, it reinforces it.)[44]

We move this toward preaching. Two churches where I
served as pastor drew heavily upon the university for their
membership. At its best, the church showed forth the oddity
that high status in the university did not necessarily represent
high status in the congregation. Graduate students chaired
boards whose membership included their dissertation advisors;
folks who had not finished college called on the provost for his
annual pledge, and the provost was as apt as the house painter
to be there repainting the kitchen or trimming the hedge. It
might have been more blessed still if we had served more
clearly as leaven in the lump; if the university itself sneaked
toward less stress on status, role, and authority. Maybe, quietly,
it did. Less quietly, the churches provided another way of
being. First Corinthians 7 helped preach us toward that.

How will new historicism help preaching?

1. We have known for a very long time that biblical texts are

not simply the products of single authors, but represent the culmination of a long process and the collation of a series of perspectives, worlds, and narratives. The new historicists would suggest that we attend to that kind of reading not only for Genesis (which we know is a composite) and Luke-Acts (which is probably a composite), but also for Paul's "genuine" letters. These were written by Paul, to be sure. But what did he draw on for his writing? What does he presuppose from his culture, some presuppositions so deep that he could not name them? What does he draw from the Christian tradition that preceded him (1 Corinthians 11 and 1 Corinthians 15 are obvious examples). But more than that, how does the "historical" Paul become the Paul of the Epistles? What does circulating individual letters to a wider audience do to their function and meaning? How does the inclusion of genuine with pseudepigraphical letters affect our reading? What about the fact that the Paul who "wrote" these letters actually dictated them, signing with his own hand only at the end.

2. Both biblical texts and Christian sermons often depend on the power of the anecdote to make connections. We tend to think of anecdotes as illustrations—a jazzier way of making the propositional point. But sometimes anecdotes are microcosms of the larger world: of our people, of biblical society, of the gospel.

3. We should not be surprised that material conditions shape stories and stories shape material conditions. The Bible —Old Testament and New—is strong on incarnation faith where the condition of the body and of the pocketbook drive beliefs and are driven by them. I recall the gnostic horror of a seminary student who had discovered that the prodigal son came home not just because he had a spiritual awakening, but because he was hungry and the cash had run out. Christian faith is a complex negotiation between hungry stomachs and hungry souls; many a hangover hangs over into life-changing repentance. Or turning it around, what good is it to say "God

bless you" to our starving neighbor while we send her on her way *(see James 2:14-16)*. New historicism helps us ground theology and preaching in the concrete physical and social realities of biblical people and of our own. Martin says it well:

> It seems to me that all arguments about priority—that one's theology is simply a reflection of one's ideology, and vice versa—are fruitless. How can we possibly know the answer to such a question? How could we ever sort out so exactly the intricate workings of another person's mind when we can never be sure why we ourselves believe certain things. Some Marxists insist that religious beliefs are nothing more than secondary reflections of a given ideology. Many religious people, conversely, believe that the true reality lies in theological statements, which then find, or ought to find, expression in one's ethics. . . . We cannot know which came first.[45]

Put another way, until that day when the conditions of social status, economic power, and legal authority disappear, and every power and authority bows before the throne of God—until that day, we live under conditions of social possibility and oppression. Our stories, our self-understandings and our theologies reflect and affect those social structures. So did Matthew's, so did Paul's, so did Ezekiel's. It may be harder to get at those social structures than to get at those of Victorian England, but our forays toward understanding them help us in our forays toward understanding ourselves, social beings all.

Canonical Criticism

For reasons quite different from those of the new critics there also has emerged in biblical studies a movement whose strategies are not entirely different from those of the new critics: canonical criticism. The leading proponents of this "method" are Old Testament scholars James Sanders and Brevard Childs.[46]

Sanders is more concerned than Childs with the canonical "process"—how texts emerge from the life of communities of faith in such a way that they become normative.

Childs is more concerned with the canonical "shape" of various texts. His approach to biblical studies includes two central claims. First, for communities of faith and for biblical interpretation in the church, it is the canonical shape of the text that counts for interpretation. We want to know what is there in the Gospel of Matthew, not in Q or some source called "M", or in some pre-Matthean version of the Sermon on the Mount. We do not care much whether an ecclesiastical redactor fiddled with the ending of John's Gospel, or the canonical Gospel includes chapter 21, and that needs to be part of our interpretation.[47] In Old Testament studies, excessive attention to the hypothetical sources J, D, E, and P may cause us to undervalue or misunderstand the shape of Genesis, the interaction of its themes. Even though historical criticism may appropriately separate the undeniable Pauline Epistles from the dubious ones (like the Pastorals), the canonical question is different from the historical question: who is the "Paul" of the canon, whose writings include both the radical freedom of Galatians and the more stable structures of 1 Timothy?[48] It needs to be noted that while the canonical form of a text is usually to be identified with its "final" form, for Childs, the issue of canonicity is really an issue of how a text functions for communities of faith, and there may well be cases where the main theological and liturgical thrust of a writing is not simply identical with the precise form it takes at the end of the editing process.

> By canonical "shape" I mean the attempt to discern those theological forces which were exerted in the shaping of the Scriptures in order to provide guidelines by which to aid its present and future readers toward its 'proper' interpretation, that is to say, one which is faithful to its true subject matter. . . . In a sense, one has to know what one is looking for in order to find it.[49]

Childs provides two examples of how the canonical shaping helps our interpretation:

1. While the book of Deuteronomy, both by its placement in the Torah and by its content, "serves as a conscious hermeneutical guide on how the preceding four other books of the law are to be interpreted, e.g., the law is summarized and actualized, thus serving as a check against both legalism and antinomianism."

2. The Gospel of Luke has been divorced from its original connection to the book of Acts and has been placed within the fourfold Gospel collection. This way Luke is properly interpreted in its relationship to the other Gospels, while Acts, now placed at the head of the body of Paul's letters, provides an interpretive guide to reading those letters.[50]

Childs' second central claim in his approach to biblical studies is this: for communities of faith, the *whole* canon counts for interpretation; so it is perfectly appropriate for Christians to read Isaiah 53 in the light of Golgotha and to read the Prodigal Son in the light of Jeremiah 31.

> The juxtaposition of the two testaments to form the Chris-tian Bible arose not simply to establish a historical continuity between Israel and the church, but above all as an affirmation of theological continuity. The church not only joined its new writing to the Jewish Scripture, but laid claim on the Old Testament as a witness to Jesus Christ.[51]

Nor does intracanonical interpretation involve only interpretation between Old and New Testament texts. Acts, as we have seen, provides a context for interpreting Paul's Epistles, and Deuteronomy provides clues for interpreting Exodus. (One can assume there can be instructive study of Mark's Gospel in the light of Paul's Letters, too.)

While in some ways canonical interpretation as practiced by Childs has some affinities with the new criticism movement, which attends to the text as we have it and not to its historical context, there are also important distinctions. For one thing, Childs comes to his readings of Scripture on the basis of an extensive reading and understanding of the historical critical questions. If anything, his is a postcritical rather than a precritical reading. As he himself acknowledges, he could not have come to his canonical readings without having passed through the historical critical questions. (And there may be some worry that disciples will skip the hard work.)[52] For another thing, for Childs, scriptural reading takes place in a context—the context of the community of faith. Scripture does not exist for itself as some kind of aesthetic object (as literary icons may do for the new critics). It serves the upbuilding of the church in faith, hope, and charity. The question about the canonical shape of the text is sometimes the question: how does the text shape faith in the church? Alternatively it is the question, How did the church (or synagogue) shape the texts and the canon in the service of their faith and liturgy?[53] That sense of the purposes of the literature is very different from the reading of texts by most literary critics— some of them biblical scholars, too.

Childs' own readings are most richly evident, not in his more encyclopedic introductions to the Scripture as canon, but in his splendid commentary on Exodus. In interpreting the central passage where the divine name is revealed to Moses, in Exodus 3:13-15, Childs first attends to the whole history of literary, source, etymological, and form-critical questions surrounding this text and its place in the book of Exodus.[54] Then he undertakes the two tasks set by canonical interpretation:

1. He looks at the canonical shape of this text, its function in the book of Exodus as we have it.

> Then Moses raises a second objection. "Assuming that I come to the people of Israel and say to them, 'The God of your fathers has sent me to you,' and they ask me, 'What is his name?' what shall I say to them?" This question has evoked

such a long history of scholarly controversy and has been approached with so many oblique questions that it is extremely difficult to hear the text any longer in its present context. Is this a genuine question? Was it something needful for Moses to know as God's messenger? . . .

Certainly in the present context Moses' question is viewed as one in a series of objections. It is part of the prophet's resistance . . . [However], clearly the people want to know more about God's intention. By requesting his name, they seek to learn his new relationship to them. Formerly he related to them as the God of the Fathers. What will he be to Israel now?[55]

Childs goes on to suggest that God's answer indicates that God knows that the question is Moses' question as much as it is the people's. In revealing the nameless name, God provides what "is paradoxically both an answer and the refusal of the answer."

The tenses of the formula indicate that more than a senseless tautology is intended, as if to say, "I am who I am, a self-contained, incomprehensible being. . . ." Rather, God announces that his intentions will be revealed in his future acts, which he now refuses to explain. . . . The reality of God will not be different from that made known in his revelation. [56]

2. Childs looks at the text within the whole context of the canon, and especially its use in the New Testament. Revelation 1:8, for example, which refers to God as the one "who is and who was and who is to come," seems to represent a development of motifs already evident in Exodus 3 and Second Isaiah *(see Isa. 44:6).*[57] Using Childs as a starting point, one can find other places where the motifs of Exodus 3 are picked up in the New Testament. As I read the Gospel of John, for instance, Jesus' use of the Greek formula *ego eimi* ("I am") sometimes echoes the Septuagint translation of Exodus 3:14, *ego eimi ho ōn.* Perhaps this is most evident in a text that otherwise seems almost an incidental detail of the narrative in

John 18. The soldiers and police have come with Judas to arrest Jesus.

> Then Jesus, knowing all that was to happen to him, came forward and asked them, "Whom are you looking for?" They answered, "Jesus of Nazareth." Jesus replied, "I am he." Judas, who betrayed him, was standing with them. When Jesus said to them, "I am he," they stepped back and fell to the ground. (John 18:4-6)

Reading this detail in the light of the canon, and especially of Exodus 3, we see how John's Gospel suggestion that the Word became flesh in Jesus of Nazareth is not only the Word who spoke creation, but also is the Word who spoke redemption to Moses' "I am."

The Gospel of John also may provide an interesting test case for our ability to do a "canonical reading" of a New Testament text. John 6:22-71 is the discussion of Jesus as the bread from heaven. Taking Childs' second principle of canonical interpretation, it is in fact impossible to read this text without paying attention to the larger canon. Jesus clearly refers to himself as the new manna, and no reader ancient or contemporary can get what he is talking about without knowing something of the story of Exodus, Moses, and manna.[58] More complicated perhaps is the question of how to read the text in its canonical shape. There seems within the passage itself to be a conflict between two ways of understanding the bread that God gives in Jesus Christ. On the one hand, Jesus himself seems to be the bread, and one receives the bread (as one receives living water) by believing in him and his words: "I am the bread of life. Whoever comes to me will never be hungry, and whoever believes in me will never be thirsty. But I said to you that you have seen me and yet do not believe" (John 6:35-36).

On the other hand, the bread that God gives in Jesus seems to be the bread of the sacrament: "Those who eat my flesh and drink my blood have eternal life, and I will raise them up on the last day; for my flesh is true food and my blood is true drink" (John 6:54-55).

Rudolf Bultmann, the most influential New Testament scholar of this century, provided a historical-critical explanation of this apparent tension: The Evangelist, who was the primary shaper of the Fourth Gospel, believed strongly in the fundamental significance of Jesus' words; he was not a believer in the sacraments or, what is also evident in this last passage, in apocalyptic eschatology. For the Evangelist, true faith was faith in Jesus, whose words provide the nourishment that manna provided the Israelites; and eternal life is not the promise of some future consummation, but of a faithful life lived now in relationship to Jesus, the revealer. Sometime after the Fourth Gospel had been written, a more "orthodox" Christian, whom Bultmann calls the ecclesiastical redactor, came along and corrected the text in order to make it conform more closely to the emerging consensus of mainline Christian faith. So statements about the sacraments and future resurrection were inserted into passages like John 6 where they had formerly had no place.[59]

A canonical reading of the text would look at the tension differently. Part of the focus of our reading would be the tension itself. We would not jump quickly into the solution of the Reformers, that true church is the church of word and sacrament. We would acknowledge that in this passage both word and sacrament are affirmed, but that they live together in a kind of uneasy dialectic. Sacramentalism does always run the danger of slipping over into magic. Preaching does always run the danger of slipping over into a wordy intellectualism, as if in Jesus Christ the Word had become argument. Word and sacrament fight with each other as much as they complement each other. The sixth chapter of John's Gospel is not so much a narrative of both Word and sacrament as it is the assertion of two theologies, each with an explicit "yes" and an implicit "no." It may be a model for the later church, both in local congregations and in the church universal, where we are always in danger of collapsing the tension between a theology of the word and a theology of the sacraments into a kind of pabulum of compromise.

A canonical reading of the text also will look at the whole Gospel of John—its love of words, its insistence on incarnation, its stress on glory, and its reminder that the glory consists in crucifixion. A canonical reading will look at the way other signs are treated—part of the story, but perhaps not the heart of the story. A canonical reading will look at chapter 21 where Christ, who fed the sheep in chapter 6, feeds the disciples and then tells Peter that he is the one to feed the lambs (John 21:15).

How does canonical interpretation help preaching? For me, it does not entirely supersede the gifts of historical criticism. Sometimes, for instance, the canonical Paul is too abstract and multiform, too separated from historical grounding. The Paul who was mad at the Galatians because they (historically, not just canonically) were insisting that males have their foreskins cut off, and who wishes his opponents might just go cut themselves a little lower—that down-and-dirty historically grounded Paul preaches concretely to the quite different but equally concrete needs of a congregation. Sometimes I actually preach better by talking a little bit about how Second Isaiah is not First Isaiah, and how the stories of Genesis 1 and of Genesis 2–3 not only complement each other, but provide alternative readings of our situation as created beings.

Nonetheless, my major testimony to the canonical strategy is one of great appreciation. It is sometimes an immense relief to attend to the text as we have it and not to think that we need to dissect it into its missing sources before we can say a word. I have read some reasonably good articles on Q and "proto-Mark"; I have never heard a sermon on either one, and even the footnotes introduced into occasional sermons have seemed to me diversions from the text given us to preach.

Furthermore, of the making of historical hypotheses, there is no end. (We have seen that literary readings may be just as diverse, but at least there is a text there that we can all agree to argue about.) It cannot be the case that my ability to preach the Gospel of John right depends on my accepting this or that hypothesis about where it originated or how long it had been since some Johannine Christians had been in the synagogue. I will suggest in the following chapters that these questions may help preaching, but that the validity of the sermon cannot depend on our finding the correct answer to those questions. If it did, all who preached on John as the most Hellenistic Gospel would have to take back their sermons in the light of new evidence, at least until next year when something else turns up.

And there is more than something to be said for preaching a text in its canonical context. Preaching is a matter of making connections, sometimes connections between the text and our lives; sometimes connections between the text and the lives of our people; and sometimes connections between the text and the social and political movements of our time. But sometimes the connections are between the text and other texts. This task is made all the easier by the fact that often Scripture has begun to do that for us. Hebrews knows Melchizedek, that odd priest from Genesis, and so does Psalm 110.

It is not altogether clear what the sign of Jonah means in the Gospels, but a good starting point to ponder that would be to read the book of Jonah. Turning it around, it is not cheating for Christians to see the verse in Psalm 2 where God calls the king his son as foreshadowing Jesus as God's son. Canonically, Matthew, Mark, and Luke all make that connection, and so may we.

It can be a kind of relief, in the midst of all the directions to preachers about reading this and attending to that, to learn from canonical criticism the first two commandments for our reading agenda:

1. Read the text.
2. Read the whole text.

I dare say, the more we do those two things the richer our preaching will be.

The World Behind the Text

W hile literary and canonical critics help us understand the world in front of the text, the social and social scientific scholars of the Bible help us to discover the world behind the text.

The assumption for these scholars is that the biblical texts are clues to the complicated social world that lies behind those texts. Sometimes they are a reflection of that world. Sometimes they are an ideological rationalization for that world. Sometimes they are an instrument of power used to gain control over the social world in which they were written.

There are probably dozens of ways of doing social scientific study of biblical books, but I set forth three.

First, there is the deep description of the social material that underlies a biblical text. Scholars seek to help us understand the economic and social structures that lie behind biblical texts: how people organized their lives and their institutions; how they earned their bread; who had what power and who had what authority; and who had wealth and who aspired to wealth. Scholars also seek to help us understand the sociology of knowledge. What did the people of the first century of our era or of the fifth century B.C.E. know or believe they knew? What did they assume so deeply that they did not even know they knew it?

(In our time, people who have never read a word of Freud

write and talk about the ego, the super-ego, and the id, and they have some notion of the Oedipus complex. People who never have read a word of Darwin either assume evolution or argue about it. Often we draw on the images of a kind of intellectual infrastructure without knowing how deeply we depend on unexamined assumptions.)

Wayne Meeks has written a social study about the churches to whom Paul wrote his letters. The book is called *The First Urban Christians*, and its insights help us rethink some texts from Paul's Letters as we prepare to preach on them. Meeks deliberately distinguishes his task from those who wish to focus on literary criticisms of the texts and from those whose writings

> depict a strange world, one that seems composed exclusively of theological ideas or compact mythic complexes or purely individual "self-understandings." If we ask "What was it like to become and be an ordinary Christian in the first century?" we receive only vague and stammering replies. [1]

While it is clear that ordinary Christians did not write the Pauline Epistles, by attending to those texts, Meeks hopes to find clues to the lives of the people for whom the texts were written—not so much as individuals, but as members of collectivities, and not so much through specific events as through typical occasions reflected in the texts. Beyond that, he seeks to find in other literature and materials clues to the nature of life in the first-century C.E. Mediterranean world.

> To write social history, it is necessary to pay more attention than has become customary to the ordinary patterns of life in the immediate environment within which the Christian movement was born. It will not do to describe that environment in terms of vague generalities: "the Greek concept of immortality," "the Roman genius for organization"; . . . nor to be satisfied with reproducing the generalizations and idealizations that aristocratic writers of antiquity themselves repeated. Rather, to

the limit that the sources and our abilities permit, we must try to discern the texture of life in particular times and particular places. After that, the task of a social historian of early Christianity is to describe the life of the ordinary Christian within that environment—not just the ideas or the self-understanding of the leaders and writers.[2]

Let me take just one of the issues that Meeks discusses and suggest some of its pertinence for our understanding of the New Testament world and, therefore, for our preaching (since we also preach to people who live in a world and not just in a church meeting house or a library). One of the persistent questions we raise about early Christians is this: What was their social class? Were they the poorest of the poor, the first-century analogue of the middle class, or perhaps even from the upper classes? Meeks looks first of all at our New Testament texts, then more specifically at the lists of names in the Pauline Epistles (some of the names have descriptions of the person named attached). While the evidence is not conclusive (we have no first-century Christian social register, no tithing records, and of course no income tax returns), it points persuasively in a particular direction:

> The extreme top and bottom of the Greco-Roman social scale are missing from the picture. It is hardly surprising that we meet no landed aristocrats, no senators, *equites*, nor (unless Erastus might qualify) decurions. But there is also no specific evidence of people who are destitute, such as the hired menials and dependent handworkers; the poorest of the poor—peasants, agricultural slaves, and hired agricultural day laborers—are absent because of the urban setting of the Pauline groups. There may well have been members of the Pauline communities who lived at the subsistence level, but we hear nothing of them.[3]

Then Meeks moves somewhat beyond his "thick description" of Pauline Christians based on the text. He draws upon a theoretical model that helps make sense of the relationship between social status and the attraction of Christianity.[4] Meeks ventures the hypothesis that many of the early Christians were "status-inconsistent." That is to say, these are people who often have high status in one aspect of their lives but have not yet achieved status in the overall society. For example, folks like

> wealthy artisans and traders: high in income, low in occupational prestige. We find wealthy, independent women. We find wealthy Jews. And, if we are to believe Acts, we find Gentiles whose adherence to the synagogue testifies to some kind of dissonance in their relation to their society.[5]

Later, having further surveyed the nature of the new Christians of Paul's community, Meeks ventures the following possible hypotheses on the reason that Christians who felt (rather than "knew") status inconsistency might be attracted by Pauline themes and conversely might influence the way in which those themes were articulated.

First, the "paradoxes" of Christian faith—new life grounded in tradition; an evil world nonetheless embraced and encompassed by God's judgment and grace—might appeal to people whose very experience was also "paradoxical," not fitting easily into this or that category. And the almost dialectical lives of these early Christians might help inspire Paul in shaping his dialectical Gospel.

The second hypothesis: "May we further guess that the sorts of status inconsistency we observed . . . brought with them not only anxiety, but also loneliness in a society in which social position was important and usually rigid? Would, then, the intimacy of the Christian groups become a welcome refuge, the emotion-charged language of family and affection, and the image of a caring, personal God, powerful antidotes. . . ."[6]

Third, would Paul's stress on the new and unexpected risk, and the freedom of the Spirit appeal to people who were already loosed from the traditional moorings of class and status?[7]

Let me clarify that in delineating the "usefulness" of early Christianity for people with status inconsistency, Meeks is not seeking to adjudicate the "truth" of Christian claims, nor here at least to discuss the ways in which usefulness and truth might interact. As preachers trying to declare week after week both that the Gospel is true and that it makes a difference, we may find this description of the early Pauline churches a help in speaking to our contemporary congregations.

In my youth as a member of a vital church youth group, I always suspected that part of the appeal of that group was that it provided a place where young people who often did not have the highest "status" in very status-conscious schools could find themselves validated and even honored.

Students of African American churches in neighborhoods where few people have social status have noted that one gift the church provides is to honor gifts that the larger society may ignore: to provide power and authority in the church that the world has never granted or acknowledged.

I teach at a university where one former colleague suggested that almost everyone on the faculty suffers from some version of the impostor syndrome. Intimidated by the university's public relations and perhaps by our own memories of predecessors and mentors more famous and, we're sure, more worthy than we, we all think the search committee that chose us made a mistake. As I write, I tremble that this very book may be all the evidence my colleagues need to discover they made a mistake in hiring me.

There is no doubt that there is a gospel to be preached to the poor, and to this we shall attend especially in the next chapter of this book. But there is also a gospel to be preached to those who fear that they are not acknowledged according to their deserts, or to those who fear that they are honored far beyond their gifts and that the day of judgment is just around the corner. In American society, where everyone pretends to belong to the middle class, how do we deal with the range between the upper middle class who are darned near wealthy and the lower middle class who are darned near poor? Probably everyone to whom we preach thinks she deserves better and simultaneously fears that she has gone farther than she had any right to go.

There is a gospel here that knows Paul Tillich's "You Are Accepted," but goes deeper: Who am I? Who is this God who calls me? What is this community of others, perhaps just as perplexed as I, who nonetheless reach out to one another in love? What is the meaning of this cross in a society driven to success? What possible meaning does the hope of resurrection have when we are trying so hard to have it all now? We are not simply Paul's Christians, but we are not so far from them, either. Sociological studies help us name them and help us name ourselves. Preaching takes place in the intersection between those namings.

Let one example provide a beginning of our thought. Some years ago, Gail O'Day noticed that a familiar passage from 1 Corinthians is not as clear as we had thought.[8] Remember that in the early Greek manuscripts of the New Testament there are no punctuation marks; there are not even breaks between the words. All the letters are in caps and just run on. HOWGOODISGOD could be a question or an affirmation: How good is God? How good is God! We cannot know without making an interpretation based on the larger context of the sentence or the phrase.

Here is 1 Corinthians 1:26-29 as we find it in the NRSV.

> Consider your own call, brothers and sisters: not many of you were wise by human standards, not many were powerful, not many were of noble birth. But God chose what is foolish in the world to shame the wise; God chose what is weak in the world to shame the strong; God chose what is low and despised in the

world, things that are not, to reduce to nothing things that are, so that no one might boast in the presence of God.

But if you just take the Greek text and change the punctuation, the first sentence can equally well read this way: "Consider your own call, brothers and sisters: were not many of you wise by human standards? were not many powerful? were not many of noble birth?"[9] Though the larger sociological context seems to point toward the first reading, the context of the passage in 1 Corinthians may cut the other way. In 1 Corinthians, it is not the "poor" Christians who bring to naught the things of this world; it is the cross. And those who are in danger of boasting are not outsiders who are put to shame by the humble origins of Christians. Those who are in danger of boasting are some of the Christians themselves, perhaps especially the "stronger" Christians whose wealth gives them status within the church *(see 1 Cor. 3:21, 4:7, 5:6, and perhaps chapters 8, 10, and 11 where those Christians with higher status seem to be eating at the expense of the lower-status Christians)*.[10]

According to O'Day's reading (and punctuation) of the text, humble Christians are not now a sign against the boasting of outsiders; the cross is a sign against the boasting of any Christian, however high his or her social status. Therefore, "as it is written, 'Let the one who boasts, boast in the Lord'" (1 Cor. 1:31).

Notice how the different punctuation and the different social description change the sermon. Now we have a text not so much for East Harlem as for Madison Avenue, for Southport, Connecticut, at least as much as for Bridgeport. The Christian gospel is the world turned upside down; outside the door of the church we park our BMWs or our Yugos, as well as our Ph.D.'s and our bonuses, and whatever other sign of status seems to mark us in the larger world. Here, the mighty are brought low, to kneel with their brothers and sisters before that paradoxical and redemptive cross that also brought our first-century brothers and sisters (masters and slaves alike) to their knees.[11]

Abraham Malherbe clearly positions himself among those who seek to describe the early Christian communities without too quickly jumping to sociological or anthropological models. His own work is based especially on a broad knowledge of Roman and Greek literature roughly contemporaneous with the early Christian communities:

> Sociological description of early Christianity can concentrate either on social facts or on sociological theory as a means of describing the "sacred cosmos" or "symbolic universe" of early Christian communities. Even though new historical information may be assimilated within old paradigms, we should strive to know as much as possible about the actual social circumstances of these communities before venturing theoretical descriptions or explanations of them.[12]

Malherbe is especially helpful in the work he has done on Paul's relationship to the church at Thessalonica. In his study of 1 Thessalonians, Malherbe draws upon a combination of rhetorical and sociological description. Rhetorically, 1 Thessalonians is a parenetic writing, that is a writing that gives moral advice. As is typical of such writing, the first three chapters of 1 Thessalonians represent autobiographical materials that "establish the basis for the exhortation in chapters four and five."[13] Like some other philosophers of his time, Paul prides himself on the fact that he works with his own hands, and this self-description provides part of the basis for his insistence in the latter part of the letter that the Thessalonians, too, ought to "aspire to live quietly, to mind your own affairs, and to work with your hands, as we directed you" (1 Thess. 4:11). Malherbe studies Hellenistic literary sources to provide a sociological description of Epicurean communities of the time of Paul.

> For the Epicureans, who formed communities, withdrawal and quietism *(hesychia)* were of the utmost importance in

attaining their goal, that calm blessedness *(ataraxia)* which could only be attained in company with others who were like-minded. They took no part in public affairs and were not concerned with receiving the approval of outsiders. It was enough for them to enjoy the friendship that characterized the sect and provided the basis for the community's means of support. Friends would naturally share what they possessed. Epicureans were severely criticized in antiquity, partly for their withdrawal from and disregard for society. They were accused of being haters of mankind and not the philanthropists they claimed to be.[14]

Perhaps with the Epicureans in mind Paul suggests a very different strategy for the Thessalonian Christians. (Christians soon would be associated with Epicureans in the popular mind.) Paul wants the Thessalonian Christians to live lives that are both appropriate to God's command and apt to win the respect of the larger world in which they live. Paul is less concerned to see the church as standing over against society and more concerned to see it take its proper place: Christians serving one another in such a way as to win the approval of the larger world in which they live.[15] The discussion of 1 Thessalonians has implications for how we preach the whole epistle and particularly for how we understand Paul's advice concerning the relationship of Christians to the larger world.

First we will read the first part of 1 Thessalonians in the light of the moral exhortations of the last two chapters. Malherbe has shown how Paul's claim to do his own work may reflect his concern that the Thessalonians also work with their own hands. Are there also other themes in the first part of the epistle that are shaped by the moral concerns of the last chapters? Does his stress on his own truthfulness and care, for example, prepare the way for the new "truth" of chapters four and five about death and Christ's coming, and for the exhortation that the Thessalonians are to "encourage one another and build up each other" (1 Thess. 5:11).

More directly in line with our concern for the social setting of Scripture, how does the situation of a minority church in a puzzled and somewhat hostile society relate to the situation of our own congregations? Much ink has been used to describe the relationship of contemporary Christians to larger American social structures. My own sense is that (as with Thessalonica) Christians will do better to do local descriptions than to fall into global generalizations. Is the mainline church dying away? Maybe not in your town. Has the church simply taken over all the values of the larger society? Maybe not in my town. Is it always a mistake for the church to take over societal values? If it is true, for instance, that "secular feminism" got to issues of the proper role of women in institutions before the church did, does that invalidate our trying to take an honorable place in a more inclusive society? (Even in 1 Thessalonians this is a tricky matter. While it seems quite right that Paul urges the Christians to take on the society's "work ethic," it is equally clear that he urges them to avoid the societal sexual ethic. *See 1 Thess. 4:3-5.*) And Malherbe's study suggests that Paul does not easily fall into either an accommodationist or an isolationist picture of the church. How does his vision speak to our own? The combination of rhetorical and sociological study helps.

Peter Lampe has written a major study of the early Christian communities in Rome using names, titles, and inscriptions on graves.[16] He persuades us that when Paul writes his letter to the church at Rome there are two different clusters of Roman Christians. The Gentile Christians are predominant in leadership and numbers, and they live in their own Gentile neighborhoods. The Jewish Christians have just returned after being banned by Claudius. In the light of Lampe's analysis, we can come to a fuller understanding of the injunction to hospitality in Romans 15:7: "Welcome one another, therefore, just as Christ has welcomed you, for the glory of God." Paul writes to both groups of Christians, who are in danger of letting their theological and cultural differences divide them from one another. That the "one another" refers to Jews on the one hand and Gentiles on the other is confirmed by the verses that follow: "For I tell you that Christ has become a servant of the circumcised on behalf of the truth of God in order that he might confirm the promises given to the patriarchs, and in order that the Gentiles might glorify God for his mercy" (Rom. 15:8-9).[17]

Preaching that attends to this text in its social context will be able to speak more directly to our social contexts. What fault lines run down the middle of our congregations or denominations? If we cannot agree with one another, can we yet learn to welcome one another? How does the command of hospitality relate to Paul's other concern for the church's purity? *(See 1 Cor. 5:6.)* What image of soteriology do we find in the picture of the Christ whose arms are outspread—not only in suffering—but in welcome?

The Christological statement is at the same time a social statement about building communities across divisions. We are justified by faith in part because such justification brings us together, while justification by circumcision or diet or philosophical acumen drives us apart.

It is not the prophets of the social Gospel alone who know that the Gospel had social roots and has social consequences. Our preaching is enriched to the degree that we understand the everyday lives of early Israelites and early Christians since the people we preach to, like us, live everyday lives—every single day.

A second way of doing social scientific studies of biblical texts is to draw models from sociology or cultural anthropology to illumine the world behind the biblical texts and therefore the texts themselves.

Robert Wilson has written a helpful guide on the use of social scientific studies for the Old Testament.[18] Wilson suggests a nuanced way in which studies of contemporary societies can help in studying ancient Israel.

The Old Testament is filled with references to various aspects of [its own] society and to the cultural phenomena which it contained. Some of these references may be unintelligible to us if we have no additional information from ancient sources or from archaeological excavations, and if we know of no comparable phenomena in our own society. In such cases, we may be able to supplement our regular sources of information by drawing on social scientific research conducted in modern societies having a social structure similar to that of ancient Israel. To be sure, each society is in a sense unique, and it would be misleading to assume that ancient Israelite society can be reconstructed solely on the basis of modern analogues. Still, if the sociological information is used judiciously so that the unique features of Israelite society are not obscured, a social scientific approach can bring us closer to the world of the biblical writers than would be possible if we relied on our own cultural experiences.[19]

Wilson's own study on prophets in ancient Israel draws on comparative anthropology to help us understand the phenomenon of the conflict between "true" and "false" prophets in Israel. Wilson's study helps us understand narratives like the dispute between Jeremiah and Hananiah in Jeremiah 28. Wilson argues that in contemporary societies where prophets and shamans are now found, the prophet gains authority from the validation of a larger social group. Central prophets are those who are validated by the majority of a community, and especially by those who have social, economic, and religious power. Peripheral prophets are those whose visions are not accepted and whose credentials are not validated by the official powers of a society, but whose prophetic gifts are acknowledged and assumed by smaller groups, themselves more marginal.

The dispute between Jeremiah and Hananiah is not only a dispute between two different prophets, it is a dispute between two different theologies. And each of those theologies has an explicable social location in the Palestine of Jeremiah's time. Jeremiah is a descendant of the priestly families who were exiled by King Solomon to the margins of the kingdom. Hananiah, probably a court prophet from Jerusalem, was a prophet accepted in his own country. Hananiah is accepted in his own country because he declares the establishment line that God has promised to protect Zion against foreign enemies, in this case Nebuchadnezzar of Babylon. Jeremiah is unpopular with the central authorities because he is heir to the Deuteronomistic theology that is associated with the northern territories of his exile. His oracles insist that judgment is coming on Jerusalem because the rulers have not obeyed the covenant declared to Moses. Because he speaks from the margins, "his oracles seem to have had no direct impact on anyone but his own supporters, and his message was strongly opposed by the Jerusalem establishment which saw him as a madman rather than as a true prophet."[20]

There are also studies that move beyond drawing analogies between descriptions of cultures and draw on further abstractions from those societies, "models" that provide a kind of interpretive grid for a variety of social settings. In New Testament studies, such books abound. New Testament scholars have drunk deep from the wells of Clifford Geertz and Mary Douglas and have poured forth an everflowing stream of new studies.

Jerome Neyrey, for example, drawing on Meeks' early work and Douglas' work, takes the anthropological model of "group and grid" to explain Christological developments in the Johannine community and in the Gospel that reflects that community.[21] The categories "group" and "grid" are used to describe a subgroup's relationship to the larger group that provides its context. In the case of John's Gospel, the Johannine church is the subgroup, and the larger group is the Jewish community out of which the Johannine group emerges. When the "group" index is high, the larger group is exerting considerable pressure on the smaller group to conform to majority expectations. When "group" is low, the larger group exerts little pressure on the smaller. When "grid" is high, the experience of the smaller community corresponds in large measure to that of the larger. When "grid" is low, the experience or values of the smaller community stand in contrast to those of the larger, parent one. Neyrey suggests that we can see in the development of John's Christology the response of a community to a crisis of identity—the persistent diminution both of "group" and of "grid." As the Johannine church finds itself more separate from the Jewish community out of which it comes and less congruent with its values, it seeks to validate itself by stressing its unique ideology. The way a Christian church stresses its unique value is by stressing the unique value of its master—now Savior, now very God.

(The more secure the community is in terms of its identity, the less it needs a high Christology to validate its community life. The more the community is threatened by rivals without and deserters within, the more it seeks to reassure itself that its Messiah is God's own son, maybe God's own self. Weak group, weak grid, high Christology.)

L. Michael White, discussing Matthew's community, argues that Matthew's Gospel shows a community caught in the stress of a sect, trying to make its way against the polemical and persuasive powers of a resurgent pharisaic Judaism. In sociological terms, a sect is defined as "a divergent (i.e., deviant or separatist) revitalization movement which arises out of an established, religiously defined cultural system, with which it shares a symbolic world view." White goes on: "A central feature of this definition is its location of the sect's origins and development within its parent culture, but where there is tension with the dominant cultural idiom, usually referred to as 'the world.'"[22] In Matthew's Gospel, the stress on the unique righteousness of Jesus' disciples becomes a way of reinforcing the identity of the marginalized Christian community, pointing out those ways in which they are different from the larger Jewish culture and how this difference is a mark of honor and not of shame.[23]

Do these interpretations help us read the text wisely and therefore preach it faithfully? Different ones of us will answer different ways. Sometimes the critics seem to find fancy names and models to show us what we had seen there all along.[24] But sometimes the text does open up in new ways. I read Matthew more clearly on the hypothesis of a "sectarian" group trying to find its way against opposition that is all the harder to combat because the conflict is between theological siblings—synagogue and church.

Certainly David Rensberger has taken the sectarian model as a clue to John's Gospel, and from that has drawn implications for our understanding of key passages in the text.

> We may think of the Johannine community, then, as a sectarian group of Jewish Christian origin, one that has distinctly introversionist features, but one that has not necessarily turned its back entirely on the possibility of mission to the world.
>
> In this setting, a dualism perhaps already latent in the group's thinking came strongly to the fore. Their Christology was also involved: if it was their confession of Jesus that had caused them to be expelled from the synagogue, their expulsion drove them to an ever more radical confession of him. Jesus became the center of their new cosmos, the locus of all sacred things. . . . His rejection by the world symbolized their own alienation, and the correct confession of Jesus became for them the touchstone of truth.[25]

With this sectarian model in mind, Rensberger goes on to explore some difficult passages in John's Gospel. For example, the saying on the Eucharist in John 6:52-57 has seemed to some (Bultmann, for instance) to run counter to the main thrust of the Fourth Gospel's stress on Jesus and his words as the bread of life. Rensberger points out, though, that within the sectarian context a ritual like the sacrament can be a means of setting the boundary between believers and unbelievers, between "church" and "world." More than that, in a context where Johannine Christians face separation and persecution, the shared relationship to Christ and to one another around the Eucharist provides a concrete means of solidarity, solidarity not just as warm fellow-feeling, but as the willingness to stand with and for each other in the midst of persecution and threat.[26]

Rensberger illustrates the usefulness of the social models for preachers. For preaching, the value of the sociological models is not in what they tell us about sociology. First, it is what they tell us about the texts; second, it is what they tell us about the nature of the biblical communities out of which the texts arose.

The test of the sociological theory is not just whether it is fascinating, but whether the text sustains it. If we know something different, or guess something different, about how John 6 works in the Gospel and worked in John's community, then the sociological models may help. Of course, finally, almost all we have is the text. We have no evidence that John's community was a "sect" apart from what we interpret as "sectarian" devices in the text, and it gets tricky when we go on to interpret difficult passages as if we had some kind of external evidence that John's is a sectarian Gospel.

Furthermore, the belief that cross-cultural studies will help, that we can understand the community behind Matthew on the analogy of more recent struggles for boundary and identity, cannot always be sustained. One would think that postmodernists, for example, would be especially suspicious of theories that link a kind of "essential" human response across centuries and miles. Do the Cargo cults help us understand Christian apocalypticism? Do African shamans help us understand the prophets? My own response to that is to take one argument at a time and ask, Does it help make sense of the text? And, of course, for the purposes of this book, Does it preach? More than that, Does it work sometimes to preach not just the text, but our best guesses about the social structures of the communities who first heard the texts?

Once I did preach a sermon drawing texts from John's Gospel and from Acts and suggesting to a congregation I loved that part of our ongoing identity crisis was that we could not decide if we were a sect, standing over against society, or a church, seeking to transform it. I would not want to preach on sociological models every week, and I did not mention Weber even once, but I think that sermon worked and helped.[27]

It need hardly be said that the theory that gets us started does not need to end up in what we say during those fifteen or twenty minutes. If "group" and "grid" make John's community come alive for you in wondrous ways, you do not need to tell your congregation where you got the idea. *Sometimes it's awfully hard to keep our faith when the world pulls at us from every side* says pretty much the same thing in standard English.

The final way of doing social scientific studies of biblical texts is to draw on a particular ideological social position to describe or to criticize biblical texts, the societies behind them, and, before long, our society as well.

Here, I think one can probably not overstate the influence of Norman Gottwald on both Old and New Testament scholars. At least the people whose works I read in this area not only reflect his thinking, but check their manuscripts out with him.

Gottwald's book *The Tribes of Yahweh: A Sociology of the Religion of Liberated Israel, 1250–1050 B.C.E.* is in every way provocative.

Gottwald stresses the story of the conquest of Canaan, which he suggests along with others before him was not so much a conquest as an internal power play, which Gottwald sees as a movement of liberation. The twelve tribes were a fairly egalitarian organization attempting to bring together a peasant society without undue stress on hierarchy. For Gottwald, the faith of Israel is not simply a projection of the social structure onto the heavens, but sometimes it comes very close to that. Here is a Gottwaldian hermeneutics or homiletic:

In our attempt to position the socioreligious nexus of mono-Yahwism and egalitarian Israelite society within the context of a larger contemporary understanding of religion, it is necessary to take our cue from the methodological insight that religion is the function of social relations rooted in cultural-material conditions of life. This entails *a rejection of forms of theology that separate religion from theology and that abstract religious beliefs from the socially situated locus of the religious believers.* The uniqueness of the Israelite religious perception lay in its discovery through social struggle that the concrete conditions of human existence are modifiable rather than immutable conditions. . . .

There is but one way in which those ancient religious symbols can be employed today in anything like their full range and power, and that is *in a situation of social struggle where people are attempting a breakthrough toward a freer and fuller life based on equality and communal self-discipline.*[28]

It is, I think, not unfair to Gottwald to say that while commentators tell us that Marxism is dead among the powers of the world it is not dead in the academy or in the ranks of biblical interpreters. Nor, I think, should it be. Whatever the larger implications of Marxist dialectic, no one who has tried to preach the gospel to the affluent on one occasion and to the impoverished on another will doubt the power of economics to drive both our desires and our beliefs. We are not only economic people, but economic people we are; and Christians ignore the power of the material at our peril—even when we preach.

At this point in our study of biblical methods and preaching, I thought it would be helpful to compare Gottwald's reading of Exodus 3—where Yahweh gives Moses the unnameable name—with the treatment of the same passage by Brevard Childs.[29] Strikingly, the index of scriptural references for Gottwald's book lists only one reference to Exodus 3 (the passage which in more text-based studies would surely be central to the focus of the Exodus story). The only verse from Exodus 3 that Gottwald treats is Exodus 3:1: "Moses was keeping the flock of his father-in-law Jethro, the priest of Midian; he led his flock beyond the wilderness, and came to Horeb, the mountain of God." The use to which Gottwald puts the text is to suggest that, as a Midianite, Jethro was probably a Kenite and that the Kenites were probably a metal-working guild who were Yahwist in religion and egalitarian in social structure, therefore appropriate allies for the struggling tribes of Yahweh.[30]

Other "key" passages from Exodus receive far fuller treatment in *The Tribes of Yahweh.* Moses' song of victory after the crossing of the sea (Ex. 15:1-8), for example, provides an important clue to the social and political issues that lie behind the biblical text. While on the surface the text refers to a victory of Yahweh over Pharaoh on behalf of the Israelites, the text more fully has been shaped by the experience of these tribes in Canaan.

> Thus, I take it that the references to the pharaoh and his armed forces are prototypical of similar lords and their armies in Canaan and vicinity.[31]

The song is sung, or recorded, in order to encourage the poorer people of Canaan to take courage against their overlords.

More recently William Herzog has written a book called *Parables as Subversive Speech*, an instructive counterpoint (or, to stay in the dialectical mode, antithesis) to the works on parables produced by the literary critics.[32]

Herzog draws from Paolo Freire and the pedagogy of the oppressed that Freire introduced to Brazil. In brief, as Herzog tells it, Freire's job was to help the peasants find a language that would be theirs and to subvert the language of the ruling classes that was used to oppress them.

Jesus used the parables of subversive speech to undermine the various elites that dominated the Palestine of his day. The evangelists tend to cover and subvert Jesus' original intention by their more "religious" reading of the parables. Herzog goes behind the text to reconstruct what Jesus may have said.

Herzog persuasively reminds us that Jesus was probably not crucified simply for being unduly pious or unusually loving. Something was going on. Sometimes Herzog seems to say: "Something was going on, and I know what it is; it was subversive speech." Sometimes he seems to say: "Something was going on, and maybe it was like this. . . ." Being congenitally cautious, I am more comfortable with the second take on his thesis.

There is much fruit here for preaching, but not for the kind of sermons we usually preach; not, I blush to say, for the kind of sermons Herzog heard me preach pretty much every Sunday for six and a half years. Here is an exercise in humility: Have one of your parishioners write a book on how preaching on the parables has gone wrong—in his hearing! Herzog says the parable in Matthew 20:1-16 on the laborers who come to the vineyard at different times is a parable on blaming the victims of oppression. Matthew has turned it into a religious parable about grace and about the last being first. For Jesus it was an economic parable and its purpose was to entice rebellion against the landowner, who originally was not God, but was simply one more typical oppressor. The landowner does not slip the single denarius to the one-hour workers secretly, but does it right out front, in full view of those who have worked harder. Outrageously he asserts his absolute property rights at the expense of justice: "Am I not able to do as I wish with what is mine?"

No wonder the workers grumble. They should grumble. Jesus set them grumbling till Matthew tried to calm them, and us, down again.[33]

That is the text Herzog wants for his sermon. Truth is, I still like my sermon on abundant grace (the last being first) better. But I do think about the text differently in part because I know that for me, these days, abundant grace is easy to affirm and abundant wealth would be tough to let go. Tenured at last with a pretty good salary, I like readings that enrich my piety but do not threaten my security.

Notice here we have strayed (or marched) far from the suggestion I made for the first strategy of preaching—to preach on the biblical text or texts. Sermons based on Gottwald's or Herzog's works will not be on the text, but on a putative world behind the text. Not on Exodus, but on the peasant uprising that was later reshaped and mythologized into the exodus narratives; not on any parable of Jesus as we find it in the Synoptic Gospels, but on a reconstructed parable that reflects what the "real" Jesus believed about the real world behind the texts. (This is not altogether different from sermons on the real Jesus who was a Platonist or a Calvinist, or whatever else we discover when we have dug far enough beneath the layers of the material actually given.)

Ched Myers, in his study of Mark entitled *Binding the Strong Man*, shares something of Gottwald's and Herzog's materialist biases, but instead of reconstructing a world behind the text—the world of Canaanite peasants or of Jesus the pedagogue—Myers argues that Mark himself writes a Gospel profoundly concerned with economic and material issues.

> Mark's Gospel originally was written to help imperial subjects learn the hard truth about their world and themselves. He does not pretend to represent the word of God dispassionately or impartially, as if that word were innocuously universal in its appeal to rich and poor alike. His is a story by, about, and for those committed to God's work of justice, compassion, and liberation in the world.[34]

Myers therefore presents subversive readings not of the sources behind Mark but of Mark's Gospel itself. For instance, his reading of the story of the widow's mite, that favorite text for stewardship Sunday, is best read not as a commendation of the widow, but as a condemnation of the social structures that reduce her to poverty and then take what little she has left for the sake of the religious establishment. Myers notes the obvious contrasts of the text (12:38-42). The widow is contrasted to the scribes "who devour widows' houses and for the sake of appearance say long prayers" (12:40). She is contrasted to the rich people who put large sums into the treasury (12:41). The contrast is presented not as a means of commending her generosity, but of condemning their greed. "The temple has robbed this woman of her very means of livelihood. Like the scribal class, it no longer protects widows, but exploits them. As if in disgust, Jesus 'exits' the temple for the final time. . . ."[35]

How do we decide whether Myers is right? We need to read the passage in the whole context of Mark's Gospel. Certainly Jesus repudiates the temple and predicts its destruction—does the sacrifice of the widow represent a sign of her exploitation or a sign of her fidelity? In giving to the temple—in all its corruption—does she nonetheless really give to God? Is the remark that Jesus leaves the temple in 13:1 really the sign of an angry departure or simply a typical Marcan transitional aside? Are we to pity the widow or to imitate her? What I like about Myers' book is that he makes me argue on the basis of the text and ask, Does he read it right?

As a preacher, both my theological commitments to Scripture and my historical commitments to particularities reinforce the claim that the test of any sociological reading of Scripture is still whether it illumines the text. It may finally be a description of the world behind the text, but the interpreter needs to show us how this text (which is, after all, what we have in hand) may plausibly have emerged from that—more hypothetical—social setting. Robert Wilson and I shared the same teachers and now share the same students, so anyone with a discerning sociology of knowledge will not be surprised that I endorse his insight:

Finally, an interpreter must apply social scientific material to the Old Testament in such a way that the text itself remains the controlling factor in the exegetical process. This rule must be followed whether the interpreter is concerned only with the exegesis of the text or is also interested in reconstructing Israelite history. The comparative material is simply used to form a hypothesis which will be tested against the biblical text. The exegesis of the text itself will confirm, disprove, or modify the hypothesis. In this way, comparative data can be used to broaden the horizons of the interpreter by suggesting new hypotheses and to assess the value of hypotheses previously advanced.[36]

For those scholars who stress the economic world behind the Bible, preaching the text in its context also takes on a new meaning. It means, above all, to preach the text in the social context we imagine it must have had. So we understand Matthew 20 not in the context of Matthew at all, but in the context of a reconstructed Palestinian social and economic situation. By implication it means to preach consistently for our social situation, not to let theological reflection lift us above the concrete material issues, especially the economic issues, that continue to drive humankind.

For both Gottwald and Herzog (as often for other sociological theorists), the social description depends on generalizations about peasant societies and on analogies drawn from quite different times and places; of independent information about social-political life in pre-monarchic Israel or first-century Palestine, we do not have nearly as much as we might want.

Both of their readings make us think about the way in which real people live in real societies. They challenge our easy ability to turn everything into spirituality and thought, even hunger and oppression. They remind us that though people may not live by bread alone, they do live by bread. Sometimes for Gottwald, Herzog, and Myers the other half of that cautionary note seems to be missing. We do not live by bread *alone.* Hope is not only hope for a dry home and the next meal; faith is not only faith in better political structures; God is not only the word we use to validate our oppression or our struggles against oppression. These scholars are not comfortable with both-Word-and-bread theology, but their "no" provides a challenge to our easy and comfortable affirmations—our ability to be like the Christians in the Epistle of James who say to the hungry and naked brother or sister, "Go in peace; keep warm and eat your fill," but do not one thing to serve the peace they invoke (James 2:14-16).

Our World and the Text

C hed Myers, whose study of Mark suggested a new interpretation of the story of the widow's mite, provides a good
transition from our discussion of reading the world behind
the text to our discussion of reading out of the world we
bring to the text. Myers argues that the strategy of main-
taining neutrality in interpreting biblical texts is an impossible
ideal; not even an ideal, but an impossibility. Each of us reads
from a "reading site"—a place that is both the result of our
social and historical locations and of our deliberate choices.

> Those doing theological reflection from a vantage point on the
> peripheries have properly focused upon the themes of libera-
> tion in the story of Exodus. . . . We at the center, however, have
> no choice but to learn to "do theology in Pharaoh's household,"
> . . . that is, to take the side of the Hebrews even though citizens
> of Egypt. There is a significant minority of Christians in the
> U.S.A. and other first world countries who are struggling to
> find a lifestyle and politics that does just that. That movement
> also constitutes the site from which I read Mark. . . .
>
> Because we understand the present crisis of empire to have
> everything to do with the ordering of power, the distribution of
> wealth, and the global plague of militarism, radical discipleship
> necessarily approaches the Bible with social, political, and eco-
> nomic questions in mind. What does Mark have to say con-
> cerning our struggles against racism? Or to find more proxi-

mate forms of solidarity with the poor while we work for justice? Or to deepen our use of nonviolent direct action?[1]

Myers' explicit willingness to name his location points to yet
another way of understanding the text. We have discussed the
world in front of the text and the world behind the text. Now
the further question arises: what about the world we bring to
the text?[2]

We might call this last family of interpretations "liberation
perspectives," which is certainly where the mode goes when
we move from Norman Gottwald to Ched Myers and William
Herzog. But the larger point that a whole host of interpreters
are making these days directly relates to the claims for interpretation we made in our discussion of Hans Georg Gadamer.

Gadamer reminds us that none of us comes to the text—any
text—without presuppositions, prejudices, and even interests.
When Norman Gottwald wrote *The Tribes of Yahweh* he was
sitting in an office overlooking People's Park in Berkeley as the
sixties moved into the seventies. Looking at liberation movements on the other side of his window, he also found them on
the other side of his text. That is not wrong or wrongheaded; it
is the human condition. It may even be that the Berkeley riots
freed Gottwald to see what was really there and what he would
have missed if he still had been in, say, Andover Newton, or
had tried to write the book in 1952.[3]

Paul Ricoeur, who has been so useful, reminds us that when
we do our interested reading of the text there are at least two
different strategies we can employ. We can use the hermeneutics of retrieval; that is, we can find in the texts or in the
worlds behind them those stories, structures, and values that
we love and wish to encourage. We can use the hermeneutics
of suspicion, meaning we cannot only ask, What is there? but
What is being hidden? In what ways is the text slanted to privilege power? What does the conscious story hide of uncon-
scious terror? (You bring a gift to your spouse and, depending

on the day and circumstance, your spouse is a hermeneut of retrieval or suspicion: "Thank you, darling" or "What did you do this time?") The great hermeneuts of suspicion, of course, are Nietzsche, Marx, and Freud, but there are lesser suspecters aplenty.[4]

(As a pertinent aside it may be well to remember that we also need to exercise a hermeneutics of suspicion on interested interpreters, including ourselves. One of my colleagues at Yale was appalled when students in his history course asked him to declare his biases. "I have no idea what my deepest biases are," he said. "The ones I can announce are almost certainly the most obvious and the least important."

I can declare my own biases as a white, middle-aged, professorial male ordained in a mainline denomination, but what are the values, fears, and hopes so deep that only years of analysis might begin to ferret them out? When I declare my wish to show solidarity with the poor, what mix of genuine sympathy and of an inverted lust for power lurks beneath my declared intention? It may be a small price to pay to cast aspersions on the methods of my teachers so that I can seem more "with it" to my students. Or, with a little bit of luck, my Bible-based condemnation of capitalism may make enough royalties that I can increase investment in my IRA. Consciously, of course, my intentions are more selfless and far seeing than that.)

A few years ago a number of scholars gathered for two annual conferences at Vanderbilt Divinity School. The focus of the conferences was precisely on the claim that interpretation depends in large part on what we bring to the text. The group published their papers in two volumes tellingly entitled *Reading from This Place*.[5]

Fernando Segovia, one of the editors of these volumes, argues that the historical and critical attempt to read texts impartially and objectively was naive because it thought it could really avoid or neutralize (the effects of social location on reading) by means of an acquired and hard-earned scientific persona. It was dangerous because in the end what were in effect highly personal and social reconstructions regarding texts and history were advanced as scholarly retrievals and reconstructions, scientifically secured and hence not only methodologically unassailable but also ideologically neutral. Indeed, given the origins and development of such constructions on both sides of the North Atlantic, the construct remained inherently colonialist and imperialistic. It emerged out of a Eurocentric setting, and, as such, it was and remained thoroughly Eurocentric at every level of discourse and inquiry.[6]

Our intuition is that this must be very nearly right. How could those of us who teach in European and American seminaries and universities not shape our readings through our own social location? Yet, perhaps because I am so immersed in the methods I have learned and I teach, it is hard for me to name even the most obvious and surface biases. Here is an attempt for today:

1. Those of us who teach Scripture in the "mainstream" of the historical-critical method do assume that we are the *main* stream. Implicitly we may believe that there is *a* right way to read texts. At the very least we think that any reading requires the indispensable attention to (our reconstruction of) what the text "meant" in its original setting.

2. Implicit in that is the claim to our own legitimate authority, perhaps even our power, as monitors over right biblical interpretation. Preachers and church school teachers are supposed to read our books in order to preach and teach aright.

3. Most of us want our methods and our sophistication to stack up against the methods and sophistication of our colleagues in other institutions of higher learning or elsewhere in our own institutions. We write often about the "scientific" study of the text, or about ourselves as "historians." This does

not mean that we are not interested believers; many of us are, but that fact often does not creep into the work itself.

4. We believe that fundamentalisms of all sorts and that claims of verbal inspiration of Scripture are not only wrong, they are socially and spiritually dangerous. Many of us are refugees from communities whose doctrines of biblical authority we have found to be repressive.

5. We tend to believe in affirmative action if that means making sure there is room in our schools and departments for women and for so-called racial and ethnic minorities, but we are nervous if the women or, say, African Americans claim that they do biblical studies differently from the way we do it precisely because they are women or African American. That is, we want feminine biblical scholars but not necessarily feminist ones.

6. Those of us who are Christians believe in the ecumenical movement and rejoice in the fact that we can cross confessional lines in our work, though we tend to prefer an ecumenical movement that includes mainline, or old line, Protestants and more liberal Catholics rather than one that reaches out more broadly.[7]

I have tried to present this list sympathetically because, of course, I sympathize with it. The social location it apparently represents is my social location; among its most articulate advocates are some of my best teachers and closest friends. But, like many of those same teachers and friends, I have noticed that other voices are asking to be heard, and I have discovered that interpretations that seem self-evident to me are not so evident to others. Hard as it is after all these years, I am trying to listen.

As I read and listen to interpreters who start with explicit acknowledgment of their perspective, I find that there are three fairly distinct strategies possible:

1. One can find in the text the signs of a more egalitarian, liberated vision than traditional interpretation has allowed.

This is a hermeneutics of retrieval from the text itself, retrieval in the mode of literary criticism.

2. One can find behind the text evidence of a more egalitarian and hopeful community than the texts themselves imply. This is retrieval in the social critical mode.

3. One can bring criticism to bear against the texts and their world where text and world demonstrate signs of oppression. This is the hermeneutics of suspicion.

Here are a few of the voices that I hear:

1. Latin American Readings of Scripture

The earliest, and in many ways the most influential, interpreters who insist on the way in which social location affects our readings are Latin American liberation theologians who have found in and behind the biblical texts warrants for their own liberating reading of the Bible. When we listen to their voices we hear the text in ways that we could scarcely have imagined.

The means by which Latin American theologians reshape our thinking are twofold. First, they interpret the texts from their position as members of "two-thirds world" countries, those who find themselves economically and politically marginalized—on edge. Second, in the Bible studies at many of the Latin American "base communities," the whole people of God join in reading and interpreting Scripture; hermeneutics moves from the experts to the community, and conversation with the text expands to include conversation with one another.

> The introduction of the Bible as written word in the base communities gave rise to a principle of authority different from that of the ancestors or that of the priest. Contact with the written text allowed the communities to insert themselves into the context of modernity, where the principle of authority is the written word—a document that is subject to criticism and not to the oral tradition of the ancestors. Whoever gains access to

the written text is no longer subject to the exclusive meaning given by the oral narrator, whose interpretive authority is grounded in the fact that he alone knows what is being narrated. Consequently, direct access to the biblical word allows for the liberation of the different meanings of the text, making way thereby for the possibility of a plurality of interpretations; such a concept, in turn profoundly alters the existing relationships of power and authority, even allowing for the construction of new models of being church.[8]

The reading is characterized as well by its communal aspect. The subject of the reading is the community, not the individual. The Bible is read not as a personal book, meant for individual piety, but as a book of the community, even when it is read individually. . . . Such a communitarian reading allows for both mutual correction and a deeper understanding of the interpretation given the text read: no one individual possesses interpretive authority; such authority belongs to all as a community.[9]

Perhaps the clearest and most concise description of the strategies of Latin American liberation exegesis is found in the essays of Carlos Mesters entitled *Defenseless Flower.*[10] In a series of essays Mesters tries in different ways to describe the presuppositions of the process by which base communities are enabled to interpret the Bible.

One way of talking about the process is to suggest that liberation or popular exegesis has three features. The first feature is freedom, a kind of sovereign willingness on the part of the interpreting community to let the text speak in their lives in a new way. This freedom is itself a gift of the Spirit. The second feature of popular exegesis is familiarity. That is to say that for the base communities the Bible is no longer the property of clergy or professors; the people themselves grow to know the stories and claims. The third feature of such exegesis is fidelity: that is, in the base communities the Bible is read as a guide to the practical problems with which people live their own lives.

Bible insights are meant to be lived out not just understood.[11]

Another way of talking about the process is to say that the three criteria for liberation exegesis are pretext, context, and text. The pretext is the actual life situation out of which the community interprets the Bible, and especially their situation as those who are not only poor, but impoverished. The context is the faith of the community, now not defined primarily as church teaching, but as the shared experience of this particular community of believers. The text is the biblical word, and it is in reading the text that "scientific" exegesis becomes especially helpful.[12] For Mesters, it is clear that scientific exegesis is helpful precisely because careful exegesis finds *in the text* just those claims that the people's lives (pretext) and the base communities (context) need to hear.

> For instance, scientific studies have shown clearly that the Bible originated in the people's life of suffering. The Bible was the product of a journey toward liberation. It originated in the lives of those in "captivity" and in the lives of those in solidarity with them. . . . It is only within the concrete world of the "captivity" of the poor that we can find the right place from which to discover the true meaning of the Bible.[13]

And yet a third way of talking about the process is to say that liberation theology attends both to the letter of Scripture and—more important—to the Spirit. Attention to the letter of Scripture tells us what a text meant for its original author in its original setting, and that is an important component of interpretation. Even more important is attention to the spirit of the Word, which shows what Scripture means for us today: "As a model, the Bible has, for those who believe in the resurrection, the authority and inspiration to reveal to us who God is, who we are, what God has to say to us, how God is present in our lives and history, and how God is guiding us through the Spirit toward Christ and the resurrection."[14]

The power of the Spirit for the interpretation of a text,

therefore, depends for Christians on the truth of the resurrection claim that Christ is not to be found only, or even primarily, in the texts that preserve a former history; he lives today
among God's people.

This last claim (concerning the Resurrection) has pertinence
not only for a liberation understanding of the limits of the historical-critical method, but pertinence for any confessedly
Christian reading of the text. The historical-critical method *by
definition* comes to a stopping point before the Resurrection,
an "event" whose claims cannot possibly fit the strategies of the
historian who moves by analogy from one event to a similar one.
Yet the Gospels, which are the starting point for the historian of
early Christianity, begin precisely where the historian has to
end. The historian's dead end is the evangelist's starting point.
This is not to say that historical-critical questions have no place
in Christian reflection on the text; quite the contrary. It is to say
that, perhaps even more than Mesters realizes, the lack of fit
between "letter" and "Spirit," and between "scientific exegesis"
and the people's faith is inevitable and even unavoidable.

In his discussion of the reading of Scripture in base communities (where he pays considerable appreciative attention to
Mesters), Paulo Fernando Carneir de Andrade also provides a
somewhat more nuanced understanding of the way in which
experience—both as pretext and as context—shapes the reading
of texts. He contrasts the different ways in which the Latin
American "poor" who are in the base communities and the Latin
American "poor" who are members of Pentecostal churches
read the same texts—out of apparently similar life situations. He
rejects the notion that one group is simply faithful and the other
alienated from true faith and right spiritual discernment.

> As formulated, this explanation seems unsatisfactory, not only
> because it is simplistic, but also, in a certain sense, because it is
> accusatory: those who do not possess the same reading we do are
> alienated; should they remove the veil from their eyes, they shall

see and read as we do. One can, however, expand on such a response by turning to an intuition present within it that has not been properly thematized: that which constitutes the "location" of reading is not the concrete social conditions of life as such "in themselves," but the interpretation of these conditions. In other words, the life that is taken to the Scriptures is not life "as it is," but rather a life that is interpreted; that is, understood within a certain cultural framework; indeed, life "as it is" does not exist: life is always interpreted life. . . . To read the Bible "with the eyes of the oppressed" means, therefore, to read the Bible from the point of view of a life that is interpreted as oppressed in social and economic terms. According to this interpretation, the relationship between the "concrete social conditions of life" and the text is no longer seen as direct but as complex: as a relationship between such conditions, the culture within which such conditions are interpreted, and the text, likewise, taken as a participant in that same culture within which the conditions are interpreted. Thus, popular Pentecostals as well as members of the base communities would be reading the text from different "locations" insofar as they belong within different cultural traditions of interpretation regarding their concrete social conditions of life.[15]

It is not just "life," but an interpretation of life out of which we read Scripture. Put somewhat differently, it takes Marx plus impoverishment plus the Gospel to enable a liberation perspective on the text. Put in another context, it is no wonder that Lutherans and Anabaptists from very similar social backgrounds may interpret their obligations to the state, say in issues of war and peace, very differently though they may live in the same neighborhoods, have attended the same schools and have about the same income. This is not for a minute to denigrate the validity of liberation interpretations or to adjudicate between the Mennonite pacifist and the Lutheran who enlists in the armed services.[16] It is to affirm with de Andrade that it takes more than experience to let us interpret "from experience."

All that is background to the freedom and beauty with which, we are shown, Latin American Christians in the base communities are able to interpret the stories of the Bible in the light of their own stories. Ernesto Cardenal has collected a number of the conversations that he recorded in discussions of Gospel texts in Solentiname, Nicaragua.[17]

Here is a discussion of the line from the Magnificat: "He has shown strength with his arm; he has scattered the proud in the thoughts of their hearts" (Luke 1:51).

Old Tomás, who can't read but who always talks with great wisdom: "They are the rich, because they think they are above us, and they look down on us. Since they have the money. . . . And a poor person comes to their house and they won't even turn around to look at him. They don't have anything more than we do, except money. Only money and pride, that's all they have that we don't."

Angel says: "I don't believe that's true. There are humble rich people and there are proud poor people. If we weren't proud we wouldn't be divided, and us poor are divided."

Laureano: "We're divided because the rich divide us. Or because a poor person often wants to be a rich one. He yearns to be rich, and then he's an exploiter in his heart; that is, the poor person has the mentality of the exploiter."

Olivia: "That's why Mary talks about people with proud hearts. It's not a matter of having money or not, but of having the mentality of an exploiter or not."

I said that nevertheless it cannot be denied that in general the rich person is a proud man, not the poor one.

And Tomás said: "Yes, because the poor person doesn't have anything. What has he got to be proud of? That's why I said that the rich are proud, because they have the money. But that's the only thing they have that we don't have, money and the pride that goes with having money."[18]

At least as we see it exemplified in Mesters and in the people of Solentiname, the predominant mode of interpretation for these liberation theologians is not a hermeneutics of suspicion but a hermeneutics of retrieval. Of suspicion there is plenty, but the suspicion is directed not toward Scripture, its authors or its editors but toward the rich, the powerful, the North Americans, and perhaps against those clergy and professors whose lifestyles and exegetical decisions reflect the biases of the wealthy and secure.

Toward Scripture there is an almost infinite openness, a trust that, when read with the eyes of faith, Scripture will reveal what God's spirit wants to reveal; the living Christ continues to speak through the living Word. In that sense at least, I think, the readings of these impoverished people to our South declare the God who "has scattered the proud in the thoughts of [our hearts and] . . . has brought down the powerful from their thrones, and lifted up the lowly" (Luke 1:51*b*-52).

2. Feminist Readings of Scripture

For me, the finest example of a feminist hermeneutics of retrieval is Phyllis Trible's book *God and the Rhetoric of Sexuality*. Trible finds themes within the text that we might have missed because we did not look with eyes that see (in this case, a woman's eyes). Trible's preface is a mission statement for the kind of interpretation I describe. "Focusing on texts in the Hebrew Scriptures, I have sought a theological voice for new occasions. . . . I do not claim that the perspectives given here dominate the Scriptures. Instead, I have accepted what I consider neglected themes and counter-literature. Using feminist hermeneutics, I have tried to recover old treasures and discover new ones in the household of faith. Though some of these treasures are small, they are nonetheless valuable in a tradition that is often compelled to live by the remnant."[19]

Then Trible provides a multitude of readings that preach beautifully, of which I cite only one.

When Yahweh wants to make a creature companion to the other creature, traditionally to make woman as companion for man, the old translation says that Yahweh will make a helper for the man. But Trible reminds us that the Hebrew word *ezer* does not ever refer to an assistant or a subordinate in the Old Testament, but to one who helps by creating and saving. Often the term refers directly to God. The woman is therefore a god-like gift, though, like the man, she is not God; she is a human helper in the image of the divine helper.[20]

The second way to practice a hermeneutic of retrieval is to find behind the text evidence of more community and openness than the texts themselves might immediately demonstrate. It has been one of Elisabeth Schüssler Fiorenza's gifts to New Testament studies to dig behind the text and find signs of early church communities where men and women met as equals.

In some of the parables of the Gospels she finds evidence of a Jesus movement—a community of Jesus and his followers—marked by reaching out to outcasts. This practice surely included reaching out to women as well as men and became a sign of hope for a church that would be fully composed of women and men—in membership and leadership alike. For instance, Schüssler Fiorenza takes the same parable that Herzog interpreted, the parable of the laborers in the vineyard (Matt. 20:1-16). Like Herzog, she describes the parable's setting in the life of first-century Palestinian peasants, but the context for Jesus *telling* the story is not an explicit economic protest against exploitation, but the practice of Jesus and his followers of including the most unlikely people at their table fellowship. "To a contemporary hearer of the parable, the householder would clearly be God, and the vineyard, Israel. The contrast between the parable's word and the actual labor practices and exploitation of the poor laborers—daily or hourly—underlines the gracious goodness and justice of God. . . . The tensive symbol *basileia* (rule or kingdom) of God evokes in ever new images a realization of the gracious goodness of Israel's God, and the equality and solidarity of the people of God."[21] Notice that, like Herzog, Schüssler Fiorenza wants to go "behind" the text of Matthew to look at social practice, both that of Palestinian landowners and that of the circle of disciples; but in this case, at least, her reconstruction is more immediately congruent with the interpretation of the text in Matthew's Gospel: social reconstruction serves more the hermeneutics of retrieval than the hermeneutics of suspicion.

Looking behind Acts and through the evidence in Paul's Epistles, Schüssler Fiorenza writes that "we recognize that the Pauline and the post-Pauline literature know of women not merely as rich patronesses of the Christian missionary movement but as prominent leaders and missionaries who—in their own right—toiled for the gospel. These women were engaged in missionary and church leadership activity both before Paul and independently of Paul."[22]

Yet Schüssler Fiorenza also stands as a model of the hermeneutics of suspicion. She criticizes the texts, and she criticizes the critics who simply accept what the Bible says without raising the question of presuppositions, without asking the difficult but necessary question, Is this Gospel reflective of the gospel? "While a liberation-theological interpretation affirms the liberating dynamics of the biblical texts, a feminist critical hermeneutics of suspicion places a warning label on all biblical texts: *Caution! Could be dangerous to your health and survival.* Not only is Scripture interpreted by a long line of men and proclaimed in patriarchal churches, it is also authored by men, written in androcentric language, reflective of religious male experience, and selected and transmitted by male religious leadership. Without question, the Bible is a male book."[23]

Remember our model of Job arguing with Psalm 8, and John's Gospel arguing with the Synoptic tradition? Sometimes faithful preaching of the text questions the text, which of course questions us, too.

Sharon Ringe, in her recent study of Luke's Gospel, takes the familiar passage of Martha and Mary and applies to it her feminist suspicions.

> The famous argument between Mary and Martha (10:38-42) is similarly ambiguous in its portrayal of women. On the one hand, the story counters stereotypical pictures of women as valued only in domestic roles like preparing meals for guests. Mary is praised for choosing to listen to Jesus instead of joining her sister's hostessing frenzy. On the other hand, however, women's traditional work is put down as of lesser value, and the woman who is clearly running her own household with all the energy she can muster is held up to ridicule. Luke shows Jesus praising the woman who sits like a mouse in the corner quietly listening to him. Unlike events where male followers learn from Jesus in order to preach the gospel and to carry out their own ministries, Mary's education is not said to equip her for leadership in the community. She simply listens and nothing more.[24]

I have never preached on this text without bringing down the ire of women (and some men) in the congregation. Their implicit hermeneutics of suspicion (what is going on here?) finds explicit voice in Ringe's interpretation.

On the other hand, in a mode more open to retrieval, Ringe suggests that the movement of Luke's Gospel is toward a world where traditional values are turned upside down and what has been denigrated is at last honored and cherished. At the Resurrection, when the male disciples have apparently forgotten what Jesus promised, the women are those who remember and those who bear witness, now to the disciples themselves (who sadly think their memory an idle tale).[25]

> [F]or Luke the point of the Gospel emerges only gradually, and at the end of it are the women who model the key to the gospel's power. At the empty tomb the women "remembered Jesus' words" (24:8), and that memory is the key that turns mourning into Easter joy. These quiet, background people—

the women who have been with Jesus from the beginning—
have not been passive objects, as at first might seem to be the
case. Instead, they have been active witnesses who in the
moment of crisis are prepared to testify on behalf of the crucified and now risen Jesus. In a dynamic that characterizes
Luke's Gospel from the very beginning, . . . categories of strong
and weak, rich and poor, insider and outsider, and subject and
object are overturned in the logic of the reign of God—God's
sovereign will for the world and for the redemption of
humankind. The women carry the story on.[26]

Antoinette Wire takes on the tough question of Paul's
injunction to women to be quiet in the church. Here is how we
find the passage in the NRSV:

(As in all the churches of the saints, women should be silent in
the churches. For they are not permitted to speak, but should
be subordinate, as the law also says. If there is anything they
desire to know, let them ask their husbands at home. For it is
shameful for a woman to speak in church. Or did the word of
God originate with you? Or are you the only ones it has
reached?)
  Anyone who claims to be a prophet, or to have spiritual
powers, must acknowledge that what I am writing to you is a
command of the Lord. Anyone who does not recognize this is
not to be recognized. So, my friends, be eager to prophesy, and
do not forbid speaking in tongues; but all things should be done
decently and in order. (1 Cor. 14:33*b*-40)

Many commentators have noticed that earlier in 1 Corinthians (11:2-16) Paul tells women who prophesy to cover their
heads, apparently assuming that women have an appropriate
role as prophets, speaking aloud in worship. In order to prove
Paul consistent, some interpreters have suggested that the
instructions for women to be silent in church is an addition by
some later scribe—someone whose views approximate those of
the post-Pauline Pastoral Epistles. It is also true that in some

Latin manuscripts 1 Corinthians 14:34-35 are found at the end of this chapter, though no early manuscript omits these verses altogether. Others have thought that perhaps it is the Corinthian men who are asking that women should be silent in church (Paul already has quoted the Corinthians to themselves several times) and that Paul here reprimands the males by asking: "Or did the word of God originate with you? Or are you the only ones it has reached?" The editors of the NRSV apparently think that this is a kind of Pauline aside, since they put the difficult verses, 33*b*-36, in parentheses.

Wire thinks, on the contrary, that Paul here reaches the climax of a concern for order which has been building since at least chapter 11. He need not be consistent across three chapters if in fact his argument is building in force and specificity. Specifically, Paul is asserting his authority over that of the women prophets who claim to have the Spirit. If they are to obey him, then they need to quench what they surely consider to be the promptings of God's Spirit. The sarcastic question about the origin and reach of God's Word (14:36) is not directed to the men of Corinth, but to the uppity women. "At this point, Paul directly challenges the prophets and the spiritual in Corinth to recognize his regulations as a command of the Lord or not be recognized themselves (14:37-38). He opens debate and cuts off debate simultaneously, leaving it up to the spiritual to decide not whether he speaks in the spirit, but whether they are spiritual enough to accept it."[27] The continuing history of the Corinthian church, as we find it evidenced in 2 Corinthians, suggests to Wire that Paul did not resoundingly win the day, that in fact it was his own authority that was soon called into question.

Notice how the strategies of interpretation work here. Wire exercises suspicion on Paul's view of the role of women in the church—a suspicion that enables her to read 1 Corinthians 11 in the light of 1 Corinthians 14 and not vice versa. (This is not to say that she does not also find more hopeful implications in other parts of Paul's first letter to Corinth.) Second, she retrieves a vision of a more egalitarian Christian community—not from the text itself—but from a community she reconstructs behind the text. As with Gottwald and Herzog, the interpretive norm is not so much what we find in the Bible but what we find behind it.

> Paul's stranglehold move on these women's voices gives us the measure of their influence in the Corinthian church. In the first place, the culminating position of his instruction on women shows how significant they are among the spiritual—any minor addendum would have come after the climactic challenge to the spiritual (14:37-38). Second, the introductory libation to the God of peace and the unspecified arguments from law and shame show that Paul knows these women are not scofflaws or objects of ridicule, but widely respected and therefore always subject to innuendo. Third, Paul's "concession" that if they want to learn they can ask their husbands at home shows that they have intellectual interests, without which it would not be credible.[28]

But this must also be said: Wire's reconstruction of the world behind the text helps me, at least, read the text more clearly and plausibly than the rather different vision of the Corinthian congregation I had before I read her works.

In her comments on the story of the daughters of Zelophehad in Numbers 27:1-11, Katharine Doob Sakenfeld combines strategies of retrieval and suspicion. On the one hand, women and men are invited to admire the daring of the five daughters who bring before Moses the question of their right to the land that would have been allotted to their late father and win their case. On the other hand, Sakenfeld looks at the larger context of Numbers and of Torah and argues that the basic point at issue was not the courage of the daughters but "the preservation of the *father's name.*" So she concludes: "This story could be heard even in ancient Israel as a story of comfort for women who would not be left destitute, but it was preserved primarily as a story of comfort for men who had the misfortune not to bear any male heirs—their names would not be cut off from their clans.[29]

How do we preach differently, hearing these voices?

We need to hear these voices. That seems obvious, but all of us have a tendency to line our study shelves with the books we bought in seminary and to return to them time and time again. If you went to seminary as long ago as I did, there were not many women voices included among the interpreters whose works we purchased.

Many of us who preach are, thank God, women. It might seem condescending for an ancient male to urge you to find your particular voices—and your eyes. In my defense, let me say that I tell that to every preacher who asks my advice. My own eyes see things they did not when I was thirty, and my voice can claim firsthand knowledge of sorrows and joys I then had only read about.

But also, insofar as it lies in you, know your *self*, not just your place. It is not the case that all women, even all faithful women, read the texts of Scripture in the same way. Some women whose preaching I have learned from think that the fatherhood of God is an inescapable given of right Christian faith and discourse (and some men, often pretty good fathers themselves, have, for better or for worse, given the fatherhood of God a sabbatical from their preaching and their prayers). I noticed in my pastorate in a church where people came from many different places (African American, Asian American, gay, lesbian, straight, single, married, younger, older, European American) that I made a huge mistake when I assumed I knew how women would read a text, or what a text would mean to "the African American community." People were always surprising me and (like me) were often being surprised by the gospel, which can make all things new. And—God be blessed—though we came from many different places, we came together to one place: a place which had a table, a pulpit, an organ and piano and—overshadowing all of it—a large wooden cross. Though it is safe to say that we read Scripture from many places, on our best days we read it toward one place: our communion with one another and with God's Spirit.

Further, if you have the opportunity, share your pulpit with preachers of the other gender (the phrase *opposite sex* seems too hopelessly bifurcated). Let your people hear other voices—in person.

3. African American Readings of Scripture

So, too, readings from an African American perspective can model these modes of retrieving and suspecting.

Renita Weems, in an article entitled "African American Women and the Bible," reminds us that for African Americans in the time of slavery the Bible was usually heard rather than read. In this aural culture, the appropriation of the Bible included both appreciation and suspicion. Weems quotes Howard Thurman remembering his own grandmother:

> Two or three times a week I read the Bible aloud to her. I was deeply impressed by the fact that she was most particular about the choice of Scripture. For instance, I might read many of the more devotional Psalms, some of Isaiah, the Gospels again and again; but the Pauline Epistles, never—except, at long intervals, the thirteenth chapter of First Corinthians. . . . With a feeling of great temerity I asked her one day why it was that she would not let me read any of the Pauline Letters. What she told me I shall never forget. "During the days of slavery," she said, "the master's minister would occasionally hold services for the slaves. Old man McGhee was so mean that he would not let a Negro minister preach to his slaves. Always the white minister used as his text something from Paul. At least three or four times a year he used as a text: 'Slaves, be obedient to them that are your master, . . . as unto Christ.' Then he would go on to show how it was God's will that we were slaves

and how, if we were good and happy slaves, God would bless us. I promised my Maker that if I ever learned to read and if freedom ever came, I would not read that part of the Bible." [30]

Weems, who tells this story, makes explicit what is implicit in much of interpretation which stresses the social and personal location of the interpreter: "Her aural contact with the Bible left her free to criticize and reject those portions and interpretations of the Bible that she felt insulted her innate sense of dignity as an African, a woman, and a human being, and free to cling to those that she viewed as offering her inspiration as an enslaved woman and that portrayed, in her estimation, a God worth believing in. Her experience of reality became the norm for evaluating the contents of the Bible."[31]

In one sense one can argue here that the interpreter is judging the Bible on the basis of her own experience. When Thurman tells the story, however, another principle is evident. His grandmother judged the Bible on the basis of the Bible. Words of grace and liberation become the standards by which to judge and, finally, to reject words of enslavement. (Those of us who love Paul will think that Thurman's grandmother may have gone too far in throwing out all of Paul on the basis of certain [perhaps deutero-] Pauline passages.)[32]

This principle of judging the Bible by the Bible did not begin with feminists or African Americans or Latin Americans of the twentieth century. One could argue that Martin Luther made a similar move when he decided that justification by faith was the central witness of the Bible. He then proceeded to devalue and even to debate discarding biblical books that seemed to contradict that central theme—notably the Epistle of James. Only the purest believer in theological truth sublimely divorced from human experience will doubt that, as with Thurman's grandmother, Luther's own "experience of reality" was a norm for deciding what was central in the Bible and what was strawy and disposable (dispensable).[33]

In the collection *Stony the Road We Trod*, using strategies of retrieval, Charles B. Copher finds within the biblical texts more African and dark-skinned people than white folk are apt to notice, and he reminds us that they are there among the cloud of witnesses.[34]

Lloyd Lewis, in a study of Paul's letter to Philemon, in that same volume looks behind the text to find evidence of Paul's rhetorical strategy just below the surface of the text. The letter makes no explicit claim about whether Philemon should free the runaway slave Onesimus when Onesimus returns to his master. However, throughout the Epistle, Paul uses familial language, language that implies mutual responsibility and mutual affection. At the beginning of the letter, Paul refers to Philemon as his brother and Onesimus as his child and then as a brother, too—both to Philemon and to Paul. Philemon is "beloved" in verse 1 and Onesimus is "beloved" in verse 16. Paul identifies himself so closely with Onesimus that he says he will take on the debts of the runaway slave. Paul does not give an apostolic command to Philemon, but engages with him in brotherly reflection: "Thus Paul has brought to light the implications of [Onesimus] being his child and the child of God in a church and community where equal status under the gospel, as shown in Galatians, is a virtue, and where an apostle, a runaway slave, and a slaveholder can be interchanged. He now leaves it to Philemon to decide what understanding of Onesimus within his household would best reflect this reality."[35]

In a perceptive study of Acts 8:26-40, Abraham Smith is explicit about his hermeneutical commitments. First, he seeks to employ "audience response" criticism, and the audience to which he attends is the first-century audience who would have heard Luke's story about Philip and the Ethiopian.[36] In this sense, Smith does what we will urge in the final chapter of this book: he broadens the notion of the appropriation of texts or stories to acknowledge communal listening. These texts drive more toward audience response than toward (individual) reader response. Second, in an almost classic statement of the agenda of retrieval, "my approach reflects an African liberationist perspective, for it posits the historical contingency and ideological commitment of texts and interpreters and, then, gives prominence to a set of political and cultural stimuli virtually overlooked by traditional studies of Acts 8:26-40, that is, Luke's characterization of the Ethiopian as a man of power."[37]

Smith persuasively shows how closely the story of Philip and the Ethiopian eunuch parallels the story of Peter and Cornelius. In each case the story narrates the illumination that comes to a "foreign representative." The Ethiopian learns about Jesus' true identity; Cornelius (and Peter) learn about God's universal kindness. What is striking is that both the Roman and the African are figures of considerable power—a centurion on the one hand and a powerful (and wealthy: notice the chariot and the book) representative of a queen. In the light of the good news declared by Acts, both of these figures of power "humble themselves before the Lukan deity's representatives and take on the quality of powerlessness, the same image associated with Jesus in the parallel speeches in 8:32-33 and 10:34-43. . . . For in the narrator's understanding of power, God's paradoxical order demands submission of the ostensibly powerful in order that they might share in the truer powerful order of the ultimate patron."[38]

Smith does not draw direct conclusions for contemporary Christian understanding, but notice that here a hermeneutics of retrieval works in suggestive and unfamiliar ways. Put differently: here is a different liberationist reading of a text. The interpreter does not read behind the text to find images of the powerless who are made powerful in God's promise, but of the powerful who are made humble. It is an important corrective to our historical and contemporary stereotyping to note that in the first centuries of our era, as now, Africans (and African Americans) may also be persons of considerable power and status. That is in itself a liberating reminder; but at least in the story of the Ethiopian the surprising gospel that humbles the powerful can humble the powerful African every bit as much as the powerful Roman. Luke certainly wanted his audience to believe that this humility was not humiliating, but liberating.

Some of the most powerful African American preaching I have heard in recent years is not directed exclusively to Christians who feel themselves powerless and marginalized, but to African American Christians who may have considerable power and responsibility. A full-fledged hermeneutics of retrieval retrieves images that challenge our easy categorizing of people and that challenge a whole range of people whose lives are always more complicated than the categories.

Notice that these scholars use the whole range of interpretive strategies to raise their suspicions and to discover hopeful memories. Lewis is a rhetorical critic, drawing on his knowledge of Paul's century epistles and their strategies. Smith draws on careful literary study of the parallels within Luke-Acts, and on the sociological categories of patron-client. These are not scholars who bring only their perspectives to the text and then find what they want to find; they bring highly sophisticated tools and—like all of us—their perspectives. I do not know if they find what they want to find; they find features of the texts that I had missed, and they persuade me that they read the texts aright.

4. Multiple Perspectives on Scripture

These readings based on the world we bring to the text raise difficult issues for interpretation and especially for the church as a community of interpretation. If we are convinced that appropriate readings of the Bible are deeply affected by our histories and social locations, how can biblical interpretation be anything other than cacophony? I speak as a Euro-American older male, and you as, say, an African American younger female. At best it seems as though interpretation becomes a matter of listening politely to each other, and at worst we construct a hermeneutical tower of Babel: we will not understand one another's speech.

Yet, in quite different ways, three interpreters of Scripture who give full attention to the perspectives we bring to reading suggest ways in which we can both acknowledge and transcend our own place, ways in which we can hold conversation not only with the text but with one another.

In 1984, Robert McAfee Brown wrote *Unexpected News: Reading the Bible with Third World Eyes.*[39] Brown suggests that our interpretation will be helped both by noticing how different the biblical world is from ours and by noticing how people from different contemporary worlds read the Bible.

> Christians make the initially bizarre gamble that "the strange new world within the Bible" is a more accurate view of the world than our own and that we have to modify our views as a result. This means engaging in dialogue with the Bible—bringing our questions to it, hearing its questions to us, examining our answers in its light, and taking its answers very seriously, particularly when they conflict with our own, which will be most of the time.
>
> That is already a complicated exercise. But it is further complicated by the fact that we must be in dialogue not only with the Bible, but also with Christians in other parts of the world who read the Bible in a very different way. . . .
>
> Significant Christian voices are being heard in the third world today. And when third world Christians listen to the Bible, *they hear different things than we hear.* . . .
>
> Third world Christians think that people like us read the Bible from the vantage point of our privilege and comfort, and screen out those parts that threaten us. They tell us that the basic viewpoint of the biblical writers is that of the victims. . . . They further tell us that they are the contemporary counterparts of those biblical victims. . . . If God sided with the oppressed back then, they believe God continues to side with the oppressed here and now.[40]

Along with other texts, Brown reads the story of the last judgment in Matthew 25:31-46. He begins by reading this "text"—showing how this passage fits in the larger framework of Matthew and how it relates to other eschatological pronouncements by Jesus in that Gospel, and arguing that this is really not a parable. Then he reads the text within the canon of the New Testament, finding in 1 John and in the Epistle of James passages that shed light on the theological significance of the Matthean story. Then he provides a theological reading of the text that might be available to any sympathetic reader (first, second, or third world), how those who do good are surprised by Christ's condemnation, and how the one who judges is also the one who has been numbered among the poor and outcast.

Finally, Brown tries to see the text through others' eyes. Here is what third world readers tell him (and us) that we might otherwise have missed. First, the distinction between the "righteous" and the "unrighteous" might just as well be translated as the distinction between the "just" and the "unjust." Not only individual goodness, but the working of justice is at stake in this passage.

Second, according to some Latin American readers, we limit the passage if we see it only as pertinent to individual charity. "Just" action on the part of faithful people involves attention to the networks of human relationships, to the systematic as well as individual ways in which people are made to hunger or thirst or go naked or face prison.

Third, reading with third world eyes, we notice a feature of the story that is easy for us to miss. It is "the nations" who are gathered before the judgment seat. Now we face tough questions: Does our nation feed the hungry and give drink to the thirsty? Does our nation welcome strangers? (Brown reflects on U.S. immigration policy.) Does our nation clothe the naked? Harder yet, how do the nations we support, say in Latin America, stack up against the nation we anathematize, Cuba?[41]

Whether we are finally convinced by Brown's reading of the

text or not, we are forced to listen to other voices and to note in the familiar story issues that we had easily passed over, perhaps because it was more comfortable to do so.[42] And we see in Brown the model of an interpreter who sees what he sees but also tries to honor the perspectives of others, however challenging those perspectives may be.

Ringe prefaces her study of Matthew 18:21-35 with a reminder about the larger context in which we all read the Bible.

> More than simply the data of one's own social location given meaningful shape, "context" is also a matter of one's active and deliberate engagement in the midst of that reality. It is thus possible for one's context to be affected—even transformed— by the realities and experiences of other persons and communities who "accompany" one and those with whom one, in turn, is in solidarity. . . .
>
> For example, women and men from Central America with whom I have worked and lived struggle daily with the economic disasters caused by the debt owed by their countries to international banking institutions based in the Northern Hemisphere. These [companions] have taught me the immediate, human consequences of decisions that to me seemed distant, abstract, and—in principle—defensible. Similarly, I have never been abused by a spouse or a lover, but women who have lived with that reality have taught me their stories so thoroughly that the syndrome of domestic violence has become part of my own awareness and therefore part of my context—the meaning— and value-filled matrix out of which I live and view the world. Put another way, while neither set of experiences is part of my story, those stories are now part of my experience, and because of them my world will never look the same.[43]

Ringe then goes on to interpret from three perspectives the teaching and the parable about forgiveness and debts in Matthew 18.

From a traditional perspective, the story contrasts the infinite forgiveness of God (represented by the king) with the forgiveness required of humans whose debtors always owe us far less than we have already been forgiven. Implicit at least is the injunction to forgive our debtors as we have been forgiven our debts.

If we move from "neutral" theology, however, to read the story from the perspective of an unspecified woman reader, the meaning of the parable remains somewhat abstract. We notice that the use of pronouns and examples suggests that in Matthew's community it is men who have power. If the enormous debt to the king is read as a kind of allegorical reference to original sin, then for some Christians that sin is especially associated with Eve; and there may be the implication that women have even more reason to be grateful for forgiveness than men, and therefore even more reason to forgive—everything.

Ringe suggests, however, that even a generic "feminist" perspective fails to anchor interpretation in a context sufficiently concrete to help. Now, sympathetically, she reads the story from the perspective of women who suffer from domestic violence. Often a woman caught in the cycle of domestic violence finds that

> a picture of God's limitless forgiveness, such as can be discerned in Matthew 18:23-35, plays into her low self-esteem and sense of inherited unworthiness. Such a person is readily convinced that if God can be forgiving of so unworthy a creature, she must in turn forgive any wrongs done to her: it is the only possible Christian response! And so she forgives her abuser . . . again and again and again.[44]

So, Ringe argues, for this text to become good news, the abused woman must first find the gospel that provides escape from violence and provides healing for her wounds, and then, from a safe place, she may be able rightly to hear a word about reconciliation in human relationships.

Finally, Ringe reads the parable from the perspective of the poor of Central America. For such Christians hearing this story, "debt" is not a metaphor for a variety of sins, or at least no theological reading can afford to ignore the real economic situation in which "two-thirds world" Christians live. "Informed by such a context, interpreters approaching the parable in Matthew 18:23-35 recognize clearly that forgiveness of 'debts' in the literal, economic sense is a necessary first step toward God's project . . . of justice and peace."[45] Ringe further suggests that, shifting the focus of the parable, creditor nations and institutions may need to imitate the king in the parable quite literally by forgiving the enormous amounts of interest they are owed if there is to be any hope for economic equity and development among the debtor nations. Then, servant-like, the leaders of the debtor nations would be responsible for promoting justice among their own people.

Notice how Ringe employs both suspicion (of male bias, of the power of creditors) and retrieval (of the hope for reconciliation, of the power of forgiveness) in a kind of dialectic that argues with the text and draws from the text at the same time.

By her reading, Ringe invites us as interpreters to entertain a variety of interpretations of key texts, an invitation that requires on our parts not only sympathy and solidarity, but active imagination—and imagination that entices us to the active quest for justice.

Stephen Reid, in his study of the Psalms, acknowledges his own "location" as an African American free church academic. However, he also calls us as interpreters to attend to the diverse social situations from which the texts can be read and prayed: "If we are to learn what it means to be human, we must do it through listening in to the Scriptures and each other's cultures."[46]

Reid's interpretative strategy requires reading a text through a series of different lenses. First, insofar as possible, from the historical perspective of the original authors or readers. Second, from the perspective provided by the cross and resurrection of Jesus. Third, from the perspective provided by social circumstance (especially here Reid includes visions derived from African American, Latino, and Asian American stories and novels). Fourth, from the perspective provided by the human circumstance, in both its generality and its specificity. (In interrogating the Psalms that claim God's kingly power to renew life, Reid sees through the eyes of an African American male student whose fear of all engagement and refusal of all hope take on different local features but represent a universal danger.)

Take one example, Reid's interpretation of one of the Psalms that celebrate the kingship of God. In the context of the community for which it was written, Psalm 72 acknowledges the responsibility of the king to carry out God's justice, at the same time the Psalm acknowledges that the "king has no power except that given by God through election, so that the justice and righteousness of the king come from God" (72:1*b*).[47] The Psalm is further interpreted in the light of the New Testament. Here is Psalm 72:9-11:

> May his foes bow down before him,
>   and his enemies lick the dust.
> May the kings of Tarshish and of the isles
>   render him tribute,
>   may the kings of Sheba and Seba bring gifts.
> May all kings fall down before him,
>   all nations give him service.

Reid interprets Matthew 2:1-12 in the light of this Psalm. Here is a foretaste of that image of the kingdom when the great kings of the earth bow down before God's anointed. But Matthew 2:1-12 also helps Christians interpret the Psalm. What we see in the light of the story of Jesus is that the one before whom the kings bow is also vulnerable; those who are exalted bow before the humble. The true anointed one lies in a manger.[48]

Reid also interprets the royal Psalms using themes from the art and literature of several cultures. African American music, such as "He's Got the Whole World in His Hands," points to the sovereignty of God as celebrated by the Psalms. Rudolfo Ananay's novel *Bless Me Ultima* tells of a heroine who courageously asserts her own agency (as the anointed king must assert agency) in order to work justice in her community. That she loses her life in that struggle plays her story off against both the assertions of Psalm 72 and the destiny of the vulnerable king in Matthew's Gospel.[49]

Finally, Reid sets his reading of the Psalms in the context of the story of one individual. The individual is African American, male, moving toward middle age. But his is also a specific, individual, and unique story—the story of shrinking trust and diminishing affection in the face of repeated loss. The very individuality of the story moves it toward universality, a striking reminder that when we interpret we do not finally interpret just as members of a particular group but as unique children of God—and we interpret for unique children of God as well.

In many ways Reid's book models an interpretive plan that works extremely well for preaching. It is a kind of hermeneutical circle from text to context to application. In practice, one can start anywhere in the circle, just so the preacher goes through the whole process and circles all the way around.

Preaching involves attention to the text in its original context. Preaching involves attention to the preacher's world, but also to the worlds of others who will be hearing the sermon. Often the best way to get at these worlds is to read literature, listen to music, and see movies or plays. Art at its best stretches the imagination to allow us to be "companions" to people very different from ourselves. But the sermon also thinks concretely about specific people—not the African American members of my congregation or even "the African American church," but Charles who is grieving over the death of his spouse, or Martha whose son seems to have drifted so far away. The more concretely we attend to the stories of the people we serve, the more broadly our sermons will touch the lives of others in the community. Reid's book models that tension.

Brown, Ringe, and Reid remind us by their modes of interpretation that the appeal to the perspective of the reader need not sentence us to hermeneutical ghettos or total bafflement. Sympathetic imagination, the ability to listen to others' readings of the text, and, I dare say, the power of the Holy Spirit can still make Pentecost out of Babel. Though we necessarily read "from our place," we still read to one another, listen to one another read, and hope that our reading serves and represents the one God who created us and our communities.

A Test Case: Peter and Cornelius

Some years ago I taught a course on preaching on social issues. Among the members of the class were African Americans, Africans (from Ghana), Euro-Americans, and one Puerto Rican of Spanish ancestry. We were about equally divided between men and women. We took as a test text for our interpretation the story of Peter and Cornelius in Acts 10. Peter is reluctant to extend the gospel and the fellowship of the Christian table to Cornelius, a Gentile. Peter goes up on the roof, falls asleep, sees the vision of a sheet with all kinds of "unclean" animals on it. A voice tells him to kill and eat the food provided; Peter refuses because the food is unclean. The voice speaks again: "What God has made clean, you must not call profane" (10:15). When Cornelius comes to visit, Peter understands that the vision refers to human beings not to beasts and says to the assembled crowd: "You yourselves know that it is unlawful for a Jew to associate with or to visit a Gentile; but God has shown me that I should not call anyone profane or unclean" (10:28).

It should perhaps be noted at the start that, as with many

but by no means all texts about authority and leadership in the early church, no women are here mentioned by name. Had we been properly engaged in a hermeneutics of suspicion we probably would have noticed that the whole story plays out between a male Gentile community leader and a male Jewish church leader.

Our interpretation, however, was divided more along the lines of "outsider" and "insider."[50] Both groups identified primarily with Peter, an identification which seems to me appropriate to the literary shape of the text where Peter is the one who is engaged in conflict and moves through enlightenment to resolution, as in many good short stories. Euro-Americans tended to read the story as I had always read it. Peter is an insider; he is blessed to be a member of the church and he is called away from his own exclusive understanding of church to reach out to those who have traditionally been excluded; in this case, the Gentile Cornelius. Our hermeneutics, I think, could appropriately be called "liberal." God calls us to reach out to those who do not normally fit the rules (as Cornelius was not kosher). We should call no outcast common or unclean. The doors of First Church are open to all.

African Americans saw the same story from a different perspective. In the "real" world—the larger world in which Peter lived—Cornelius has all the power. He is a military commander of the right class, race, and authority. Peter and the church are outsiders, a struggling minority holding the faith in a hostile environment. Peter has a much more difficult question than whether to be nice to outsiders—the oppressed is asked to welcome the oppressor. The very community whose identity is defined over against the dominant culture is now asked to welcome a leading representative of that culture. No wonder Peter is suspicious. Now the issue is not just whether the Holy Spirit can help insiders be nice to outsiders in a kind of noblesse oblige. The issue is whether Christians who feel themselves marginalized in a multitude of ways have the obligation to show Christian hospitality to the very ones who marginalize them. (How long will Cornelius' humility last when it becomes clear that he gives the largest pledge of anyone in church and that Peter's raise in annual compensation depends precisely on keeping this Roman happy?)

Neither reading was wrong.[51] All of us understood the text differently and more richly because we were subjected to the alternate readings. All of us understood each other differently and more richly because together we had wrestled with this text.

By now one of my biases has become clear. Readings that acknowledge the place of the reader and of the reader's community liberate the text. They liberate the text from a kind of mystical lodge of right interpreters—the ones who know what the text really means. They liberate the text from some of the inevitable limits that any of us bring just because we are who we are and we see as we see. They may liberate us from something of our bondage to old habits and familiar readings by requiring us to imagine ourselves as very different readers. They may liberate us from our isolation by inviting us to find new companions along the way, companions very different from ourselves. In my experience, such readings do not invite us to rampant relativism, or to abandon loyalty to Scripture, much less to Scripture's God. They help us see the text afresh, but it is really the text we see. The text helps us see each other afresh. Together, before the text, we get a brighter glimpse of God.

In the end, the Women's Bible, the Liberationist Bible, and the Interpreter's Bible must still be our Bible, or more daringly, God's Word, or how shall we speak together? More important, how shall we worship together?

The History of Effects

A word also needs to be said about how we hear from our place in the history of interpretation—our confessional place and our chronological place. None of us comes to the text innocent of history or of tradition. Sometimes knowing that can enrich our interpretation and our preaching.

The biblical scholar who has most helped us think about the "history of influence" or "history of effects" in interpretation is Ulrich Luz. He acknowledges his debt to Hans Georg Gadamer.

> The philosopher H. G. Gadamer has introduced the concept of "history of influence" [*Wirkungsgeschichte*] as a dimension of the hermeneutical task. As Gadamer sees it, we do not assume the position of neutral observers or critics vis-à-vis the texts which shape our history; rather, we ourselves are indebted to the history which they have brought about. Accordingly, to become aware of the history of influence of a text means to become aware of how we ourselves have been shaped by the text. This means at the same time that we must become aware of our own position vis-à-vis the text, a position which is never simply a neutral one. Only the person who becomes aware of his/her personal, ecclesiastical, and societal position vis-à-vis the text, and learns to assess what he/she owes to the text can adequately appropriate historical or literary critical interpretation for a present-day understanding of the text. Awareness of the history of influence of a text leads to a present-day understanding of the text which moves beyond the distancing and neutralizing effects of scientific exegesis.[52]

For Luz, the history of influences is not only a study of texts, but of the influences of biblical texts "on piety, prayers and songs, dogma, Christian action and politics, and literature and art."[53]

Luz looks at Matthew 25:31-46 and claims that interpreters have suggested three major ways of reading this story of the last judgment. Most popular in recent years has been the "universal" reading of the text. The king calls all the nations (all people) together and judges them not on their theological beliefs but on their charity toward those in need. This is a reading that has enormous appeal in a time when Christians are often moving away from a dogmatic insistence on the exclusive claim of Christian believers on God's eternal mercy, and provides a way of recognizing appropriate behavior even among those who had no idea, or no concern, to serve Christ by serving the "least" of his brothers and sisters. Among the "influences" of this reading is the famous story by Leo Tolstoy, "Where Love Is, There is God," where Martin the shoemaker unknowingly welcomes Christ by serving others.[54]

For most of the centuries between Matthew's Gospel and the nineteenth century, the dominant interpretation of this passage is what Luz calls the "classic interpretation." The story is told primarily to encourage Christians to care for the "least" of their brothers and sisters; the address is above all to the church in terms of its responsibility to fellow-believers who suffer from deprivation. The influence of this reading is seen in the legend of Martin of Tours, the catechumen soldier who gave half his cloak to the poor (presumably Christian) beggar at the city gate of Amiens and that night saw Christ himself clothed in that half of Martin's cloak.[55]

The third, "exclusivist" interpretation, has become prominent (I think more in exegetical than in homiletical circles) in the latter part of this century.[56] A number of scholars have noticed that the "brethren" in New Testament discourse and especially in Matthew are not the needy in general, but Christians. Further, the "nations" who are gathered may well represent the unbelieving pagan world (as a translation of the Hebrew *goyim*), and the question posed is, How will the larger world respond to needy Christians, especially to needy Christian missionaries?[57]

In a careful reading of the text in the larger context of the Gospel of Matthew, Luz argues that the "classical" interpretation is in fact the most persuasive reading of the text for Matthew's audience. The discourse comes at the end of a series of sayings directed not to the nations, but to the disciples—who stand as kind of surrogates for the church. As elsewhere in the Bible, in Matthew final judgment is judgment for all, not least important for Christians. And, in fact, the "least" in Matthew's Gospel probably do represent first of all the needy Christians, especially itinerant missionaries. More stable Christian communities are enjoined to care for these hungry and sometimes endangered brothers and sisters.[58]

> The location of the readers is the same as in 10:40-42: They are the ones who are being questioned, not those whose claims are now finally being confirmed (i.e., "the least"). They will remember that in their own congregation love has grown cold, lawlessness has gained the upper hand, and there is in their midst hatred. . . . Accordingly, when they read v. 40 they will not afterwards identify themselves with the "least of the brothers" as though they themselves no longer stood under the judgment of the Son of man. Rather, they know that they themselves have been challenged just as much by Jesus' proclamation as all other humans and that their own congregation can be just as much the field of the devil as the rest of the world. *(cf. 13:38-39.)* [59]

On the whole, Luz provides a persuasive reading. However, alerted as we are by the other interpreters we have studied in this chapter, I note that the place one finds addressed in Scripture often reflects the place where one stands in the "outside" world. Luz, like me, and most of the interpreters he cites could never be confused with the "least" among Christians nor among the citizens of the earth. We are the establishment church and academic "liberals" whose charity must be enticed by a stern Lord. Perhaps were my story more like that of more marginalized Christians I would read the story less as a call to my charity and more as the stern demand of justice against good-hearted disciples who have good-heartedly neglected the needs of people like me. Certainly Luz would want to include in his study the "influence" of this story on people who are not white, bourgeois, and "first world."[60]

Most radically, while Luz exegetically affirms the basic correctness of the "classical" interpretation, theologically and ethically he wants to help us make the transition to the more "universal" reading.

> We have spoken of the fascination of the "universal" interpretation of our text, which is a central evangelical interpretation for many people—and for myself as well—because it opens up fundamental areas of life to Jesus' gospel of unrestricted love. This interpretation is not tenable on the basis of the Matthean text. . . . But attention to a text according to the history of influence seeks to take seriously that the sense of an old text can become new for readers in a new situation. The question is therefore: Is it theologically permissible to interpret a text against its original sense, if the sense which emerges is centrally gospel for today's recipients and at the same time helpful to them in their own situation? I would like to answer this question in this instance—not always!—with a "yes," and to point out on the basis of the biblical text the reasons and the limits of this "yes."[61]

Luz provides three reasons for suggesting the legitimacy of moving the text—from its original sense—to a more universal implication. First, the larger context of Jesus' ministry, teaching, and crucifixion points toward universal love, love even for the enemy. Jesus' vision is broader than Matthew's and can sometimes warrant our expansion of Matthew's text. Second, because in this text itself the church is included in the general judgment (without special status or favor), there is a tendency in the text against any kind of exclusive attention to Christian claims; and the universal reading picks up on this tendency, though the tendency is more implicit than explicit in the judgment narrative. Third, Luz asks the Augustinian question, Does this interpretation "produce love"? "Yes! It provides eyes to rediscover the poor of the world, the non-Christians, and, yes, even God himself in such a way that the love of which the text speaks becomes a reality."[62]

However, Luz wants to argue, the text is not simply an accidental starting point for this broader interpretation. It continues to present and re-present Jesus as the one who calls us to judgment and who enables us to stand. "Jesus is rather that one who provides new eyes which allow one to see and experience poor fellow humans and God in new ways; and the text is the source of a power which allows one to stand fast in the final judgment."[63]

In a striking way, Luz moves beyond asking what "effect" or "influence" the text has had to arguing, theologically, what effect it should have. The story of Jesus and the criterion of love are held up as central to what makes Scripture good news, and, as I read it, preachers are permitted to move beyond the narrow exegetical sense of a given text (at least of this given text) to find the good news to which the text may point but which lies somewhere beyond it.

This is both liberating and troubling: liberating because it provides a kind of move beyond texts that are uncomfortable to preach; and troubling because it may provide too easy an out from those texts whose power lies partly in their power to trouble.[64] Put another way, it is essential in this conversation with the text that at the end of the day the text's voice still be heard loudly, clearly, and, so far as possible, in its own accents. Otherwise it is not a conversation; I just hold my monologue in the presence of that disturbing, but blessedly silent, visitor from the past—Matthew's Gospel.

Whether I am finally persuaded by Luz's reading of Matthew 25, or by his final intentional misreading, I am entirely persuaded by him and Gadamer that adequate interpretation of a text includes attention to the contexts in which that text now works and has worked through the centuries. Those contexts are not only scholarly, exegetical, or written; a whole world impinges on our reading, at least of the texts we know the best and preach the most eagerly.

I cannot read Isaiah 9:6 without humming Handel's *Mes-*

siah. Notice that what I hum is *Messiah*, not "a musical setting for Isaiah." I know that when the prophet spoke his prophecy he did not have *Messiah* in mind, nor even Jesus as Messiah. In the context of the libretto Handel used for *Messiah*, Isaiah points toward the Messiah, and there is no question who that is; it is Jesus. In preaching we do well to attend to the pre-exilic or exilic prophecies and their editing. We also do well to attend to the worlds (like Handel's work) that have borne those traditions to us.

African Americans (I hope all Americans) read Exodus in the light of emancipation. "Go Down, Moses" is not just a song about Egypt thousands of years ago; it is about the United States a hundred and thirty years ago. What if Gottwald and others turn out to be right, that the issue behind Exodus was peasant uprisings in Canaan and not Hebrews suffering under the lash of Pharaoh? That is a good thing to know, but it is still a good thing to know that we have had our own Pharaohs and our own lashes in this country. If we let that connection go, we eviscerate some remarkable preaching and some priceless songs of praise.

I try a small example of the history of effects. As I work on this book, I often listen to the local classical music station, or at least play it as background for my thoughts. Twice in one week the station played the *William Tell* Overture by Rossini. The overture "originally," of course, was for a rather melodramatic opera based on the story of William Tell, the Swiss patriot who shot the apple off his son's head with a well-placed arrow. But for children growing up in this country from 1940 to 1970 it was also the theme song for the radio (and then television) program *The Lone Ranger*. You may hear the music and think "William Tell and little Tell," but if so, you are unique among American listeners of a certain age.

Twice the public radio station acknowledged the history of effects. On day one, announcer number one cried out as the overture came to an end, "Heigh-o Silver, Away."[65] On day two,

announcer number two said softly, but distinctly, as the overture came to an end, "I'm not going to say it." A whole community of listeners was formed, not just by Rossini, but by
Rossini in the context of the masked man and the white horse.

In the church, the connections are usually more organic and
just as firm. "For Unto Us a Child Is Born" does mean Jesus
when we sing it the last Sunday before Christmas. "Miserable
person that I am, who will deliver me from this body of death"
does mean *simul peccator et justus* when I come to the prayer
of confession. "Inasmuch as you have done it to one of the least
of these" does help drive the annual "Inasmuch" offering for
the homeless in our town, even if Luz is right that originally
the text had more to do with intra-Christian affairs.

I know there may have been two Magi or twenty-two;
Matthew does not say. But the people have seen all those
Christmas pageants and last year Charlie, Luke, and Timothy
were the Kings. Three of them. Count them. Maybe Luther
got Romans 7 wrong as an interpretation of Paul and right as
an interpretation of Christian existence.

Sometimes we preach the text against all the interpretations
that have tugged and pulled it into a shape the original authors
or editors would never recognize. Sometimes we preach the
text as it has been re-formed and reapplied by Augustine or
Luther or Calvin or Wesley or Gardner Taylor or Barbara
Brown Taylor. Either way, we need to nod to the ways in which
the text carries its context in the minds and hearts of our people. And when we say that we are preaching the text rather
than its interpretations, we need to remember that the next
generation will be able to show how much we tugged and
pulled that text according to our own unacknowledged and
invisible predilections, too.

Historical Criticism Revisited

At the beginning of chapter 2, I noted that, like many of those who read this book, I began my exegetical and homiletical career learning that variety of interpretive strategies called "the historical-critical method." Krister Stendahl's essay on biblical theology in *The Interpreter's Dictionary of the Bible* set the agenda for our work: first find out what the text meant and then ask what the text means.[1] Stendahl acknowledged from the start that the biases of the historian are bound to affect the reconstruction of the history, but nonetheless he was sanguine about the possibilities of objective history:

> All this naturally calls for caution; but the relativity of human objectivity does not give us an excuse to excel in bias, not even when we state our bias in an introductory chapter. What is more important, however, is that once we confine ourselves to the task of descriptive biblical theology as a field in its own right, the material itself gives us means to check whether our interpretation is correct or not. To be sure, the sources are not extensive enough to allow us certainty in all areas; and the right to use some comparative material, while disregarding other material as irrelevant for our texts, gives further reason for uncertainty, but from the point of view of method it is clear that our only concern is to find out what these words meant when uttered or written by the prophet, the priest, the evan-

gelist, or the apostle—and regardless of their meaning in later stages of religious history, our own included.[2]

While it will become evident that I am not ready to abandon Stendahl's hopes altogether, from two sides the reign of historical-critical confidence has come under siege. A number of critics think that the historical-critical method simply mistakes the nature of interpretation. A number of critics (sometimes the same critics) think that the historical-critical method, even if it succeeds in finding out what a text "meant," is not much help in showing us, including us preachers, what a text now means.

Advocates of all the critical methods we discussed in chapters 1, 2, and 3 of this study have questions about the adequacy of historical criticism as it has been taught and practiced in our seminaries and religious studies departments.

Literary critics complain that historical critics put asunder what God, or at least the author of a biblical book, has put together, undervaluing the unity and the movement of the text as is. Searching for sources and shards, the historical critic tends to lose the forest for the trees. Looking behind the text for community context or authorial intent, the historical critic misses the most obvious center for interpretation—the text itself.[3]

Canonical critics similarly remind us that the text the church affirms and preachers preach is the text we have, not some hypothetical source behind it, and that a reading of that text is what counts for faith and practice. Of course it is what the *text* meant that Stendahl asks us to understand; but in practice the quest of historical critics often has been to understand Ur-Mark, Proto-Luke, or the elusive Q, not Mark, Luke, or the Sermon on the Mount. Brevard Childs and others recall us both to the canonical text and to overtones and relationships among texts within the canon in ways that go beyond strict attention to what an original author may have "meant."

Reader-response critics tend to think that literary critics (and by extension, one assumes, canonical critics) give the text itself too much autonomy. Interpretation takes place at the intersection between reader and text. The text does not signify except in the conversation with particular readers, and interpretation is neither the attempt to dig behind the text nor even to dig in the text, but to talk with the text and see what emerges as the conversation. Another way to make this point is to say that for such critics Stendahl's disjunction between what the text "meant" and what it "means" does not work. Meaning is always an exchange between text and interpreter—in the present.

Biblical interpreters who speak self-consciously from a particular social perspective (Latin American liberationists, feminist critics, African American critics) argue that the presumed ideological neutrality of the historical-critical method is itself an illusion. The historical-critical method flourishes in privileged European and American universities among highly educated white males. Little wonder, say these critics, that this so-called objective method rationalizes oppressive and patriarchal strains within biblical texts, or fails to see the more revolutionary countermovements within Scripture itself or behind it. The historical-critical method is skewed in favor of the status quo, and the quest for truth is made hostage to the quest for tenure.

Sometimes (though by no means always) ideologically related to those perspectival critics whose criticism has a strong liberationist bent are scholars who draw heavily on social-scientific models to interpret biblical texts. The problem with the traditional historical-critical method has been in part that it is too narrow a reading of history, one that does not ask about the deeper social structures underlying the biblical stories. So Norman Gottwald suggests that behind the conquest stories in the Pentateuch lies a history of peasant uprisings directed toward a more egalitarian society. William Herzog draws on the theories of Paolo Freire to suggest that the Gospel narratives tend to spiritualize and ecclesiasticize Jesus' original preaching, whose purpose was to enliven and empower the oppressed.[4]

Postmodernist critics hold that all objectivity is illusory and that every interpretation is as much a "text" as the text it is interpreting. The job of interpretation is to play with the text to see what enticing possibilities emerge. Then, if the interpreter is lucky, his or her interpretation will be published and other interpreters can "play" with it.[5]

Yet, another group of critics holds that it is not so much that the historical-critical method is mistaken, but that even when undertaken successfully it is virtually useless for the life of faith and the practice of the church. Walter Wink, at least at an earlier part of his career, threw up his hands in dismay at the sterility of the whole historical-critical enterprise. Monographs abounded: did faith, hope, or charity?[6]

Nonetheless, and even taking all these criticisms and doubts into account, there is both a descriptive and a prescriptive word to be said for the historical-critical study of Scripture.

Descriptively, the historical-critical method is the presupposition of (almost) every other method of biblical study we have described. To begin with, every interpretation requires either that we learn to translate our text or that we find a translation we can trust. The hard philological, comparative study that enables our translation is itself a kind of historical criticism.

Literary criticism wants to recapture the shock and power of the story. That is all to the good. But we do not know that it is shocking for Jewish listeners to learn that the helpful neighbor is a Samaritan unless we know who the Samaritans were and how they related to the Jews. That is an issue of historical criticism. As Childs practices canonical criticism, the interpretive strategy seems to depend on historical criticism as a discussion partner. His arguments are frequently of a "not that, but this" variety; and it is hard to know, in our time at least, how the canonical claim could be advanced except in contrast to particular historical-critical readings. (If you have always assumed that all of the book of Isaiah was written by the eighth-century prophet Isaiah, you have no stake in a discussion of how Second and Third Isaiah fit into the canonical book.)

Of all the literary critics, only the poststructuralists or the deconstructionists sometimes look as if they could do without historical criticism altogether. One essay puns on the name Mark and the mark of the cross, ignoring the fact that the Greek name *Markos* does not mean "a mark" or "a sign" at all.[7] But most of the time what is deconstructed has been constructed first; the fun is in undoing what your more traditional colleagues are doing. Without the foil the foible fails.

Social criticism, especially in its thick-descriptive mode, is clearly a legitimate offspring of the historical-critical method. Those who use models drawn from sociology or anthropology still have to check their hypotheses against the same norm more traditional critics do: against the text. If the textual evidence supports the argument about grid and group, so be it. If not, the model has to be sacrificed to the quiddity of the text. Those who write out of the ideology of protest draw heavily on historical reconstructions. If it turns out that Jesus was aspiring to economic upward mobility and by "kingdom of heaven" referred exclusively to future individual bliss, Herzog's thesis about the parables is in trouble. If the confederation of the twelve tribes turns out to have lacked all hint of egalitarian structure, Gottwald's vision fails.

Perspectival criticism that admits its interest and reads the text interestedly nonetheless reads the text historically. Even if the answer to the question, What did the text mean? depends in part on who is looking for the answer, historical-critical studies are a crucial component of meaning. Using the hermeneutics of retrieval, Phyllis Trible finds in the text themes that have been undervalued. Lloyd Lewis looks at Philemon with a set of questions dictated in part by an African American perspective. But for his conclusions he depends on a study of epistolary rhetoric and of first-century social circumstances: the old tools are used to a new purpose.[8] The feminist hermeneutics of suspicion depend on a testable historical thesis, namely that much of the canon was shaped by males and around male-centered themes and interests. This is a case that can be evaluated in historical-critical ways. We can broaden the method, enrich its nuances and variety, but we cannot really escape the method without escaping history.

Not only do we all depend on the historical-critical method, we all should do so. We should do so because of the Great Commandment, to love God and to love neighbor. The God we love is still not only the one whose Word became words, but the one whose Word became flesh. To affirm incarnation is to acknowledge history, and to acknowledge history is to admit the validity of many of the old historical questions. The neighbors we love are not only those from other places; they are those from other times. The Yahwist and Mark are our neighbors in the communion of saints, and simply to use them as mirrors for ourselves or as excuses for our own creative ingenuity is to violate our Christian commitment. Cross-culturalism is not just synchronic; it is diachronic, too. We are called to love the community that shaped the Psalms and the community that read the Pastoral Epistles, even if they are very different from ourselves. We are commanded to love them enough to seek to understand them.

Furthermore, I affirm the value of the historical-critical method for preaching. My hypotheses about those old writers and their communities join in conversation with my assumptions about my world and the community in which I preach.

Even the older form of literary criticism, source criticism, can help. In Year A of the Revised Common Lectionary, we preach on one version of the beatitudes; in Year C, another. There is a difference between *Blessed are the poor* followed by a *woe* on the rich, and *Blessed are the poor in spirit* with the *woe* omitted *(contrast Luke 6:20, 24 with Matt. 5:3)*. We will not want to preach on the theology of Q (or at least I will not want to), but some attention to sources helps us see how Matthew and Luke understand the eschatological blessing. Such a study may help us to ask, in this present crisis, What word speaks blessing most powerfully for my people? What word warns us faithfully of woe?

It may be my shortsightedness or slavery to habit, but I know strategies for preaching on the three Gospels that assume that Mark was a source for Matthew and Luke. I would have to think my sermons differently if I became convinced that Matthew was the earliest Gospel after all. Maybe one (of several) reasons I resist that thesis is that I doubt that it would preach as well, which may just be another way of saying that hermeneutically it may not work.

Form criticism relies on a considerable amount of guess-work. What method does not? But much of what form criticism helps us guess about is the community behind the text. What were their interests? What were their needs? This is useful because we also preach to a community in front of the text—our people. Take Mark 2:1-12. Form criticism tells us that, here, two genres merge and clash: a miracle story about a healing and a controversy story about forgiveness. The pericope names the tension: "Which is easier, to say to the paralytic, 'Your sins are forgiven' or to say, 'Stand up and take your mat and walk'?" (Mark 2:9). What church does not know that clash? Heroic prayers for healing are sometimes granted, sometimes not. Forgiveness is sometimes easier to believe in than health but sometimes so much harder. Form criticism invites us to preach the clash, first-century and almost twenty-first century, too. (This is not the same as saying that form criticism invites us to preach about form criticism. There is a distinction between what helps get the sermon going and what goes into the sermon itself.)

Redaction criticism asks, What does the author do with the sources at hand? Assuming that Luke used Mark's Gospel, notice how the passion narrative differs from that of the source. In Mark's Gospel, Jesus' last words are "My God, my God, why have you forsaken me?" The centurion standing by says, "Truly this man was God's Son" (Mark 15:34, 39). Luke presents much the same story, but the dialogue changes. Jesus' last words are "Father, into your hands I commend my spirit."

The centurion's words are "Certainly this man was innocent" (Luke 23:46-47). What theme does Mark's Gospel here portray? Remember that the centurion is now telling us what Mark himself told us in chapter 1. This is Jesus, Messiah, Son of God. The fulfillment of that promise comes only through suffering. What theme does Luke's Gospel portray? We discover that in the second volume of his work, the book of Acts, Luke tells us that Stephen's last words were much like Jesus' last words: "Lord Jesus, receive my spirit" (Acts 7:59). Stephen, like Jesus, becomes an example of faithful piety in the face of persecution, a model for the Christians of Luke's time. We do not want to preach the footnotes from the redaction critics, or even necessarily to tell the congregation that Luke had read Mark (at least we don't need to tell them that every week). As preachers, however, we watch how the redactional details shape the story that re-presents the gospel and shapes our sermon.

Rhetorical criticism anchors itself more strictly in the texts. How do letters work, for instance, to convince or to persuade? Many years ago, Paul Schubert showed us that Paul, like many other ancient letter writers, used the thanksgiving sections toward the beginning of his letters to indicate the themes of the letters to come.[9] In 1 Corinthians, the stress of the thanksgiving is on spiritual gifts as opposed to knowledge, and the proper use of each. In Philippians, Paul gives thanks for genuine love and the prayer for wiser love. In Galatians, there is no thanksgiving at all. Instead of "I thank God for you," Paul writes, "I am astonished at you" (Gal. 1:6). Of course they noticed, just the way you noticed when your about-to-be former beloved stopped signing the letter "Love" and switched to "Warmly."

Let me illustrate with three test cases the usefulness of the historical-critical method for preaching.

The interpretation of the dialogue between Jesus and Nicodemus in John 3 depends in part on how we decide to translate what Jesus says to Nicodemus: "You must be born again," or

"You must be born from above" (John 3:7). Suppose we read the text in the light of what the historical critic J. Louis Martyn says is going on in John's Gospel. At the center of the Gospel is John 9 in which a blind man is cast out of the synagogue for his confession of Jesus. Martyn says that the story gives us a context for the entire Gospel. Jewish Christians are being forced to choose between their faith and their comfortable and comforting relationship to synagogue and family. Those who confess Jesus are being excommunicated, set loose.[10]

In the light of that historical hypothesis we read the Nicodemus story. Nicodemus is a Pharisee, a leader of the Jews. He comes to Jesus by night because he wants to be invisible, at least to the other members of the synagogue. Nicodemus is told that he must be born *anōthen*. This is a Johannine pun. In part it means that Nicodemus must be born from above; and that theme is in Jesus' conversation about how the Spirit blows, giving gifts from above. In part, or likewise, the term means that Nicodemus must be born again. But in the context suggested by Martyn, this does not just mean a conversion experience for Nicodemus; it means a *conversion* experience. Nicodemus must become like a baby, naked, all over again. He must give up his power, prestige, and status in the community.

Notice how historical criticism helps preaching. It helps us understand that the pun is a pun (in Greek now, not in English). It provides a situation to help us understand the text in context. The situation may have links to our situation, too. How much preaching about being born again really calls the listener to give up everything and start over, like a newborn child? We tend to preach "being born again" as part of a theology of glory; in John's Gospel it is part of the theology of the cross—or to look at the whole of John's Gospel, it is part of a theology of the cross *as* the only genuine glory *(see, for instance, John 12:20-26).*

Literary criticism also can help our sermon preparation. Do we notice how the symbols of light and darkness work in John's

Gospel? Nicodemus comes by night, and by night Judas goes out. Jesus is the light of the world. John the Baptist is not the light but bears witness to the light.

Social analysis also may help. Jerome Neyrey drew on anthropological models and related the Christology of John 3 to issues of group-and-grid identity; and that, too, may help us read the text. But again we will need to check the model against the text itself.[11] Historical-critical method is not the only tool for our preaching and it may not be the dominant one, but it provides a check, a text, and a tool: Is it really this text we are preaching and not some edifying figment of our enthusiastic imaginations?

Patrick D. Miller, writing about biblical prayers, notices a similarity between Psalm 85 and Psalm 22. In both, the complaint of the psalmist turns to thanksgiving.

In Psalm 85, the reason for the transition is made clear:

> Will you be angry with us forever?
>   Will you prolong your anger to all generations?
> Will you not revive us again,
>   so that your people may rejoice in you?
> Show us your steadfast love, O Lord,
>   and grant us your salvation.
>
> Let me hear what God the Lord will speak,
>   for he will speak peace to his people,
>   to his faithful, to those who turn to him in their hearts.
>   (Psalm 85:5-8)

Miller suggests that in the very liturgy of the faithful there came a moment when the priest, or leader, spoke a word from Yahweh, a word of assurance that turned complaint into rejoicing. Here, the moment for that divine assurance is clearly indicated by the language and tone of the psalm itself. "The psalm thus suggests that at some point in the midst of the prayer for help, or whatever ritual or liturgy may have accompanied it, those praying expected a specific word of response from God communicated to them in some manner. The particular content or character of that response is peace *(shalom)*—well-being, safety, security."[12]

What is visible in Psalm 85 may be invisible in Psalm 22. The shift from lament to praise may well indicate the fact that in the worship of the community a similar word of assurance has been spoken, a word that we do not have in the psalm itself, which is, after all, the script for the community, not for the person who speaks the words of assurance on behalf of Yahweh. "The claim that God has heard the prayer (Psalm 22:21*b*, 24) is so sure and the reversal of the psalm so sharp that one can account for all of that only on the premise that a word of assurance and salvation has been received from the Lord, an oracle of salvation."[13]

We tend to undervalue the Psalms as material for sermons, using them gladly elsewhere in the liturgy but seldom using them as a central resource for preaching. Yet, critics such as Miller help us see the centrality of the Psalms to the life of Israel (and certainly to the life of faithful people now) and help to show the way in which some of the Psalms themselves enact a whole drama of salvation: lament/assurance/rejoicing. This is not a bad structure for a sermon.[14]

Historical-critical hypotheses can help preachers in conversation with literary and canonical interpretations. Looking at the whole canon, we remember that Mark shapes his story of Jesus' passion to show forth echoes and allusions to Psalm 22. Thinking like critics of literature, we notice that Mark's Gospel ends with a long silence (like the silence between Psalm 22:21*a* and 22:21*b*). Is this the kind of silence in which only a word from God can provide the appropriate assurance that will lead to Easter joy and the confidence of believers?

In Year C, the lectionary assigns Hebrews 10:5-10 as the Epistle reading for the fourth Sunday of Advent. Hebrews is not easy material for any preacher to tackle. Its oddness makes us realize what perhaps we also should realize of other biblical texts: the world of the writer is very different from our own. (The Gospel text is the Annunciation and Magnificat.)

The text's "foreignness" is evident in at least three ways. First, we notice the way in which Old Testament texts are assumed not only to refer to Jesus but to have been spoken by Jesus; Psalm 40:6-8 is simply put in his mouth without apology. Second, the whole argument depends on a contrast between the old sacrificial system and the new; neither of these seems particularly intelligible to contemporary Christians, at least not to congregations where I preach (or to the preacher). Third, there is clearly some kind of play on "will." Is it God's will or Christ's will that is at stake here (10:10); in either case, how does that "will" relate to sacrifices? I am helped in my understanding by the almost paradigmatically historical-critical commentary by Harold Attridge.

Attridge suggests that the contrast between ritual and conscience has parallels both in the prophetic literature and in Hellenistic philosophy of Hebrews' time. What is new in Hebrews is the insistence that the sacrificial system is transcended, not first by the individual conscience of religious people, but by the conscientious sacrifice of Christ.

Attridge also notes the ways in which Hebrews modifies the Septuagint reading of the psalm, which itself probably tries to modify and clarify the Hebrew. In verse 10 is the pairing of God's will and Christ's body. That it is God's will that establishes Christ's sacrifice reminds us of the transcendent nature of that sacrifice. That it is Christ's body that is sacrificed reminds us that the transcendent promise is made incarnate in this man, Jesus. In 10:10, Hebrews for the first time uses the double name—Jesus Christ: Christ, the divine will now made incarnate; Jesus, the embodiment of that divine will, as the sacrifice both human and heavenly.

Furthermore, the introductory remark of Hebrews 10:5 establishes this text as an appropriate one for Advent. "Consequently when Christ came into the world, he said. . . ." Heretofore Hebrews has been especially concerned with Christ's heavenly role as high priest: he has entered into the sanctuary. Now the author turns more directly to his earthly role as sacrifice: he has entered into the word, into human history; the Word has become flesh.[15]

Now we can perhaps see how for Hebrews Jesus Christ fulfills the promise of the Magnificat. God's help for "his servant Israel" and God's fulfillment of "his mercy according to the promises he made to our ancestors" are found not only in the birth of this Jesus but in the sacrifice. His willingness to give himself as sacrifice not only fulfills the promises to the ancestors, it shifts those promises to a whole new basis, a different "system" of atonement, a radically new piety. In his sacrifice, heaven and earth are joined for the redemption of the world.

Hebrews is a difficult text and makes for difficult preaching, but the historical-critical study makes its themes clearer and helps us see analogies both to other biblical texts and to our own time. What are the structures of piety by which we evade the sanctity to which Christ has called us and which he enables? How do we in our bodies, in our historical contingency, honor the one who did God's will in his body and whose coming Advent honors and awaits? (I think as preachers we also will want to ignore the lectionary's limits and preach the whole paragraph from Hebrews 10:1-10.)

At a time when many American scholars and theologians want to downplay the historical-critical method, it is helpful to hear a testimony from Latin America, where historical-critical questions still play a crucial role in the Bible studies of the base communities:

> By means of biblical courses, pamphlets and primers, the findings of contemporary exegesis have been made widely available to the base communities, so that their reading of the Scriptures can bring together exegetical knowledge and research with the culture and life of the people. This is a very important element of this reading, and one that is not always properly emphasized, insofar as it shows that the reading of the

base communities is not just spontaneous, as indeed no reading ever is. At the same time, it cannot be said that such a reading is a mere reflection of contemporary biblical exegesis. Such exegetical tools and results are . . . like eyeglasses that allow the eyes to see better. The eyes—that is to say, the vision—are and must continue to be those of the people who direct their sight and their eyes wherever they see fit. It should be emphasized as well that just as so-called scientific exegesis plays a part in the reading of the base communities, so does this reading make a significant contribution to scientific exegesis insofar as it opens up new meanings and possibilities in the text.[16]

The historical-critical method still helps our preaching because we are still historical people. As Scripture moves typologically from exodus to exile, and from Abraham to the Roman Christians, we too move from exodus and exile, and from Abraham and Rome to the present—still caught on a journey toward Canaan or toward home, and still setting out by faith, or else we would never set out at all. All of the new methods enrich the treasure house, but sometimes it is not so bad to bring forth from the kingdom's treasury what is old as well as what is new. Those old and old-fashioned biblical critics can teach us still—and enrich our preaching.

What Shall We Say to This?

There are some conclusions we can draw from this study, which attempts to be more study than conclusive strategy for preaching.

1. We hold fast the centrality of the text. Of course it is not the Bible we preach but God in Christ. Yet the safest—and most daring—way to discern and proclaim God in Christ is to see and proclaim through the lens of specific biblical texts. Norman Perrin's cautionary word about the limited values of structuralism still provides an appropriate criterion for different strategies of interpretation: does this method help us understand the text more clearly and, I would add, preach it more persuasively?

The world behind the text may sometimes be an appropriate source for our preaching: our reading of what life was like in the first-century urban churches, for instance; or our guess about psalms of ascent and their relationship to the temple at Jerusalem; or even our theories about what Jesus "really" said before Matthew, Mark, Luke, and John got hold of it. But the farther the hypothesis gets from the text, the less persuasive it is historically and the less useful theologically.

The world we bring to the text—and the world of our people that we bring to the text—is an essential part of preaching. There is no interpretation without conversation. But the text questions us as sternly as we question it. The testimony of generations of faithful people—and the testimony of the Holy Spirit—suggests that this odd collection of texts we study is not just interesting literature or historical evidence, it is canon. The church and its interpreters in every age bring our own questions and concerns to the Bible, but it is also the Bible that shapes the church, makes us church.

2. We acknowledge the inevitability of perspective. Everything I have read from feminist and liberationist interpreters reminds me that I bring my own biases—more gently, my own perspective—to every text I read. Sometimes that is a problem because it closes me to other readings and to possibilities in the text itself. Sometimes it is a gift, because the text does have something to say to people whose stories are very much like mine.

It is good both for me and for my congregation if I can acknowledge those biases, but I know enough of the history of interpretation to know that my deepest biases are probably hidden from me. Other contemporary interpreters will be able to help discern my angle of vision. But future interpreters will discover what all of us in the late–twentieth century assumed so deeply that we never had to say it—including assumptions that our spiritual children and grandchildren will find at best quaint and at worst abominable. (Our ancestors, steeped in patriarchy, did not say to themselves, "Isn't sexism grand?" They did not even know the term.)

What is most powerful about the variety of perspectives on biblical texts is that different readers help us discover features of the text that we would have missed without the readers' help. I read the story of Adam and Eve differently because of what Trible saw there, and the Epistle of Philemon differently because of what Lloyd Lewis discerned in its rhetoric. We all do well to be wary of interpretations that say just what we know the interpreter believed before he or she got to the text. But we do even better to listen to interpretations that help us rethink what we already believed before we got to the text or heard anyone else's reading.

3. A variety of modes are appropriate to the variety of texts and occasions, and to the various needs of our people. There is no clear rule to say what strategy is most appropriate to what text. I have already argued that historical-critical tools are unavoidable and appropriate as one step in the process of interpretation.

Perhaps literary criticism is most helpful in reading the most evidently "literary" texts of Scripture—the Gospels, narratives, poetry. A literary reading of Leviticus or 2 Timothy is harder and less fruitful.

Social criticism can help us with understanding the context of most texts and therefore with understanding the texts themselves. My own testimony is that I have learned most about the relationship of prophet to people, and that of Paul to his communities. In part this is because there is more evidence of those relationships in the texts themselves than there is, say, in Mark where we have to guess at the nature of the community that read his text, or Job where the story seems less anchored in concrete situation. We have texts about kings and people accepting or rejecting prophets; and we have a strong sense of what Paul thought the Corinthians were saying (probably including quotations from them), though, of course, Corinthian Christians might not have accepted the accuracy of Paul's description.

Prophets and Paul also help us think about issues crucial to contemporary communities of faith: the relationship between word and deed; the authority of proclamation in its relation to the validation by the people; and the limits of diversity and the promise of unity. Social analysis of the text often works well with social analysis of the congregation.

There is no way to avoid canonical criticism when Matthew quotes Isaiah or Paul quotes the Psalms. The canonical question faces us squarely then, and woe to us if we simply hedge it week after week. Other weeks, there will be a less clear connection between our text and other canonical themes (or between the texts the lectionary has assigned), and there may be no point in searching for elusive connections out of a laudable commitment to the unity of Scripture.

Perspectival interpretations help us appreciate the perspectives of the people in the pews. Every congregation includes males and females; we pray for churches of considerable economic and racial mix. Hearing other voices in the books we read helps us hear other voices in the congregations we serve. Furthermore, there is no reason we can't structure those occasions to hear the other voices of our congregations straight out, not through books that serve as surrogates for their own interesting and complicated perspectives. Even poststructuralism may sometimes set free the mind, if not the heart. For the preacher, I do not believe that deconstruction ought to be the end of the expository process but that it can be a part of it.

4. When we preach, we will keep in mind whole texts

and not just pericopes. Pericopes are both gifts and problems. They are gifts because they are manageable, and they are problems because they are manageable. John's Gospel is considerably less easy to control than the Nicodemus story (though that, too, keeps bursting out of the bounds of our exegesis). Exodus 3 is full of hope, and Exodus 16 is full of fear. Before we can deal with the pericope we need to know the book of which it is a part (and in time the canon of which the book is a part). I like many of the guides to lectionary preaching and write for some of them, but I wish we would put them down occasionally and read a major study of John or Exodus before dashing back to the few verses chopped off for this week's sermon.

5. What we preach is the crucified Christ. And we preach the risen Christ, too: Christ's ministry remembered and his presence celebrated in the church; and the Christ anticipated by the prophets and again by John of Patmos. What we preach is not the text but the Christ to whom the text points. If our sermon holds up Christ, we have done all that can be asked. Still, and last, how best can we know it is Christ we hold up and not the figment of our wishes or our fears? Start with the text.

6. Scripture speaks not only from faith to faith, but from people of faith to people of faith. Part of our responsibility is to acknowledge the gift of particularity, the particularity that makes Amos different from Micah, and Luke different from Mark. Also, the particularity that makes First Church different from Second Church, and Maude who is grieving in the third pew different from Annie who is rejoicing among the choir. Six months after my arrival at a new parish, one of the church leaders accosted me and said, "For six months I've been saying to my wife, 'He knows his stuff.' This morning I said, 'Now he knows us.'" Let the preaching begin.

Preachers' Questions for Biblical Scholars

We have been looking at the ways in which biblical criticism may help us preachers. We have been considering questions that professional critics may help us ask of the text. There is, however, an equally important issue that I think is raised too seldom in conversations between preachers and biblical scholars. What do we as preachers have to ask of the critics? I raise this question not simply as an academic exercise but in the confidence that many biblical scholars want to know what might be helpful to us in our ministry of proclamation. I want the scholars to hear from us preachers. As we make our lists, I want us to discover what we might value and what we might hope. I would hope that professional biblical critics and preachers alike might acknowledge that preparing a sermon is often the richest Bible study of all.

We preachers can ask our questions, and we can vote with our purchases. Maybe we can buy fewer quick-fix books for this or that parish problem and save more money for the substantial work that moves us to reconsider how we preach on this biblical book or that—how we treat one central theological or social theme or another.

Here are some issues we can ask biblical scholars to attend to, or concerns that we can bring to the conversation:

1. We want biblical scholarship to pay attention to not only the history of the text, but the history behind the text. We know that our faith is not built on historical scholarship. We are impressed by narrative criticism and by Hans Frei's reminder that Christ is presented *in* the story. Nonetheless, when we preach, we want to be able to talk about what God does in the world, not just what God does in the story. And (if that is possible) we want to assume some congruity between the Jesus of the Gospels and the Jesus in whom Word became flesh, not just text.

We can put the issue of historicity more clearly negatively than positively. There are many historical questions on which the evidence will shift without enormous effect on belief. But what would threaten in our faith? What is the historical bedrock on which our faith depends? If we discover that that old book *The Passover Plot* (Hugh J. Schonfield [London: Hutchinson, 1965]) is accurate and that Jesus did not die and live again but that he dozed off or was doped and then revived, we are in trouble. If we find scrolls where the disciples admit that they stole the body and made up a story about resurrection, we are in trouble. If we discover that Jesus was dragged kicking and screaming to the cross, that is a problem for us. If we discover that he detested sinners and tax collectors and that his disciples, in a stunning example of reaction-formation, portrayed him exactly as he was not, then our faith is under siege.

It is not just because I spend much of my professional life worrying about the New Testament that my examples are all drawn from the Gospels. As Christians, we revere Scripture because it points to Jesus—not only and not exclusively but persistently and persuasively. If we discover that the witness to him is all wrong, then our faith is wrong as well. Note clearly: I expect no such disconfirmation. As a preacher, I just want to remind scholars that while history is not all important, it does count, for faith as well as in the academy.

On the other hand, what historical scholarship can give us is very limited indeed. Albert Schweitzer showed how descriptions of "the historical Jesus" fit the theology of the people describing him. Nowadays, those who love poetry and conundrum make Jesus a poetic puzzler. Those who want to liberate us describe him or his social setting in such a way as to warrant liberation. We do sometimes find the history we bring with us, and the text can be a better critic of our subjectivity than our historical reconstructions are apt to be.

The deepest things we want to say about our God and God's Christ—creation, redemption, resurrection, final glory—are not subject to historical study in any straightforward way. As a preacher, I strongly believe that biblical scholarship needs to honor historical questions but not be obsessed by them. It is Scripture, not the history behind Scripture, that grounds our faith. But Scripture makes claims about what the real God does in the real world. What seems to many of us the popular obsession with what Jesus "really" said or did may represent in part a perfectly legitimate intuition that the God of creation needs to act in the world and not just between the covers of a book, however central that book may be to our faith.

The apparent interest in finding out more about the historical Jesus (evident among so many laypeople) may be testimony to the legitimate human need to root our faith in "facts"—even when we know quite well that faith cannot be reduced to any set of data. We want scholars to help us strike a balance between book and history.

2. Closely related, as preachers, we would like for scholars to help us understand proclamation in the Bible itself. Not much has been done to look for preaching in the text since C. H. Dodd drew the distinction between kerygma and didache and tried to find a model for early Christian preaching behind the sermons of the book of Acts.[17] A study of preaching in Scripture would look again at the sermons in Acts, whether they represent apostolic preaching or Lukan reshaping of such preaching for his time. Such a study would look at the rhetorical strategies of the prophetic books, as well as their social location and theological claims.

Even if we decide that Jesus' parables were a pedagogy of the oppressed, they were also a kind of proclamation. How did they function as preached? as a source for preaching? We get some clues in the editorial additions apparently provided by the early tradition or by the evangelists.[18] Some have claimed that sermons lie behind Hebrews and 1 Peter. Maybe that is an unprovable claim, but we can do rhetorical analyses to see how these Epistles function homiletically. The hope is not to find a new formal fundamentalism, so that once we decide how the prophets or early Christian orators shaped their sermons we would do just the same. Rather, such a study helps us understand our conversation partners and, therefore, understand our part in the conversation.

3. We want biblical studies that help us think about how people understand texts in their relationship to communities, not just in relationship to the individual scholar sitting there with lexicons, concordances, and grammars (or nowadays with the latest computerized Bible tools). Reader-response criticism and the other forms of literary criticism sometimes seem to postulate the lone reader sitting at the desk and wandering through the Gospel or the Psalms. But most often we hear the Gospel when we sit together in church, and together we speak or sing the Psalms. How about moving from reader-response criticism to congregation-response criticism? We can guess that biblical texts were usually spoken or read aloud to the communities. How do these factors (aloud, communities) help us interpret the texts?

So, too, we tend to preach not to one person alone, or even to the whole congregation one by one. David Buttrick's book *Homiletic: Moves and Structures* reminds us that we preach to the gathered people and that what we preach helps shape who they are as a people.[19]

Form criticism was a start, and books about orality are another start. We are not only people of a book; the book belongs to a community of people. Both biblical scholarship and homiletics can help us understand this more powerfully.

4. Closely related, we need biblical studies that are linked to liturgical studies. One way of thinking Bible is to think Matthew and then Mark and then Luke and then John; or then Luke-Acts and John and the Johannine Epistles. We can think canonically, or we can think historically. But we can also think liturgically. How do texts relate to each other in the worshiping life of the community? More broadly, how do word and sacrament really come together; what tensions, what synthesis, in our own communities of faith? How do word and sacrament interact in crucial biblical texts?

Again we might start by looking for liturgy in Scripture. Studies of the Psalms have been immensely helpful here. How about studies of hymnody in the New Testament, too: the choruses in Revelation, the doxologies in Paul's Letters?

Then we need scholars who acknowledge that we use Scripture in a liturgical setting. The model for most scholarly writing has been the classroom. The scriptural books are there as resources for literary or historical study in a college, university, or seminary. But, in fact, for most people the texts function within worship most of the time. The Gospel writers did not know that week after week their texts were going to move us toward the Lord's table, but we know that. Hearing the texts in our context is partly to acknowledge that these are words that function in holy places and holy times, and to move us toward sacraments and then, we hope, toward service. While God did not invent the lectionary, many of us praise and proclaim God by using the lectionary. We do not need more books and journals telling us the mysterious secret that ties the four texts for this week together. We do need more nuanced discussions of how texts echo and play against each other.

I can make the same claim from a different angle. When we come to worship, especially, much of Scripture is performative language, not descriptive language. It acts as much as it refers. "Blessed are the poor in spirit" blesses. So does "Bless the Lord, O my soul." Neither text is talking about benediction; each is doing benediction. We need help with the way in which scriptural words act among us, not only to inform but to bless, chasten, and redeem.

5. Everything I have written in this book about the world we bring to the Bible suggests that this is an hon-

orable time to attend to confessional readings of Scripture, as we appropriately attend to women's readings or
African American readings. Of course such readings are
implicit all the time, even when we pretend they are not.
Rudolf Bultmann demythologized in ways that were at least as
Lutheran as they were Heideggerian, and John Meier studies
the historical Jesus by asking particularly Catholic questions of
the text.[20] In my youth, Catholic biblical scholars were busily
insisting that there was no special approach to the text that
came with being Catholic. Now, Liturgical Press publishes
Sacra Pagina, a series of commentaries by Catholics for
Catholics; the series richly informs the rest of us who listen in
on Catholic conversations. The Word Biblical Commentary
series does something of this for more evangelical Christians.
Would Presbyterians or Methodists or Episcopalians find
enough special about their perspectives to do the same?

**6. Some biblical scholars are attending to psychology
again.** Gerd Theissen draws on different psychological models
to help interpret different aspects of the New Testament.
Robin Scroggs has written about Paul in terms that have a
therapeutic impact and about the larger theoretical relationship between psychological and theological themes. In the
same book that bemoaned the bankruptcy of the historical-
critical method, Walter Wink found wisdom and motivation for
biblical study in the insights of Carl Jung.[21]

There is, of course, a legitimate concern that the gospel has
been turned into therapy and that churches have turned in the
twelve apostles in favor of the "Twelve Steps." Nonetheless,
every age needs to find the conversation partners to help it
speak the gospel for the healing of nations and for the healing
of souls. We can shake our heads in bemusement at the popu-
larity of Thomas Moore and M. Scott Peck, and checking the
best-seller lists may not be the best way to discover the long-
ings of our people's hearts. Those lists, however, do provide

one clue to the depth of that longing and to the terms that popular writers can use to speak to that longing.

I would argue that the relationship between psychological and theological categories is metaphorical rather than translational. Salvation is not *just* mental health, and sin is not *only* guilt. Nonetheless, as with good metaphors, the therapeutic categories can provide a purchase on what may seem to be the more remote theological ones. Only those who believe that the language of Zion exists in a vacuum, like the jargon of some ancient mystery religion to be taught to initiates alone, underestimate the power and value of making connections—not conflations—between theology and psychology (as every pastor knows who ever marched forth from seminary full of theology's Holy Otherness only to confront endangered marriages, depressed deacons, and driven adolescents). It may seem a little ironic to use Freud, the great master of the hermeneutics of suspicion, as our ally in a hermeneutics of retrieval, but God has been known to work through ironies before.

7. As preachers, we want to encourage biblical scholars to think about ethics, and we want ethicists who think about the Bible. As Christians, we often fall into dispute and disrepute because we take our positions fervently and bolster them with a verse or two from the Bible. There are more excellent ways. There are studies of ethics in the New Testament, or the New Testament communities, by people such as Wayne Meeks and Victor Furnish.[22] There are studies like that of Thomas Ogletree that show ways to link biblical texts to contemporary strategies of ethical reflection.[23] There are contemporary claims for the gospel, based on a particular reading of the New Testament as countercultural by people such as John Howard Yoder and Stanley Hauerwas.[24]

Christians who see Christ and culture related more paradoxically than do Yoder and Hauerwas will hope especially for books that help us with the middle ground between impossibly broad principles and impossibly narrow imperatives. How do we think faithfully about abortion? war and peace? economics? We do not need more lists of proof texts. We do need to pay considerable attention to how the texts might inform our thinking, our praying, our preaching, and—pray God—our acting.[25]

8. As preachers in middle-class America, we need books that help us attend to liberation perspectives while admitting that most of us are not among the poor or the marginalized. In a way, this is a canonical plea. Scripture may show a preferential option for the poor, but it is clear that the relatively rich and relatively powerful also are figured there. Demands are placed upon them, judgment is pronounced, and sometimes mercy is shown. How do these biblical bourgeois— or even aristocratic—become sign and judgment for us?

This is also a claim about conversation, that term overused even in this book. If interpretation is real conversation, then no perspective is ruled out ex cathedra, not even the perspectives of white males in their mid-fifties resting on their laurels, or their pulpits, or their tenure. It is also a plea for help with making the distinction between solidarity and make-believe. Sitting in our isolated offices "keyboarding" on our computers, we write about God's preferential option for the biblical poor and then drive past the real and contemporary poor on the way to our comfortable suburban homes. My guess is that most of the poor do not think that poverty is as romantic as we think, and that their own preferential option would be to live at our economic level. Who are we really? What do we know? What is the difference between enjoying our guilt and owning our responsibility?[26]

9. As preachers, we are glad for studies that help us look beyond pericopes to chapters, and beyond chapters to whole books of the Bible. At a time when we cannot presuppose much biblical literacy on the part of our people, we need books we can use and books we can recommend. We need books that are savvy about historical-critical questions but not so bogged down in history that they forget to say a word of hope for today. And not so bogged down in chapter 12, verse 12, that they forget that 12:12 is only a transition between the miracle in chapter 11 and the humility in chapter 13.

10. As preachers, we need books that take us where Ulrich Luz suggests we need to go—through the history of interpretation. As a Baptist, I am particularly aware of the heretical view that God jumped from the New Testament to us, with no interpretation in between. We are all heirs of Augustine and Teresa and Luther and Calvin, and other local saints and heroes whose reading of the text colors our own. We read the text better when we read it through the ages and not just across them.

In some ways all of this is to say the most obvious thing of all. As preachers, we need biblical scholars, or we need to be biblical scholars who are theological. We can say two hundred thousand things about the biblical texts. One hundred thousand of them will be true, and twenty thousand will be interesting. But if God is not God, and if Scripture is not God's witness, we are mostly serving antiquarian interests. There is nothing wrong with antiquarian interests, but for preachers and for those who want to help preachers, and for the people who wait each week on the word of God, they will not suffice. What the text says is not as important as whom the text presents, or re-presents, or entices us to love, or invites us to question, or hides from us until another day.

That is to say, for us—those who have no time for neutrality—biblical scholarship, like preaching, serves the gospel (the good news) through which God delights and redeems the world that God has made.

N o t e s

Introduction

1. The discussion of the threefold form of the Word of God is found in *Church Dogmatics*, vol. 1, part 1, trans. G. A. Thomson (Edinburgh: T&T Clark, 1936), 98-140.

2. See *Church Dogmatics*, vol. 1, part 2, ed. G. W. Bromiley and T. F. Torrance (Edinburgh: T&T Clark, 1956), 719.

3. See Thomas G. Long, *The Witness of Preaching* (Louisville: Westminster/John Knox, 1989), 45.

4. Hans Georg Gadamer, *Truth and Method*, trans. Garrett Barden and John Cumming (New York: Seabury, 1975). Tracy's own hermeneutical work, which is in part in conversation with Gadamer, is *Plurality and Ambiguity: Hermeneutics, Religion, Hope* (San Francisco: Harper & Row, 1987).

5. *Church Dogmatics*, vol. 1, part 2 (1936), 718.

6. Hans Frei, *The Eclipse of Biblical Narrative: A Study in Eighteenth and Nineteenth Century Hermeneutics* (New Haven and London: Yale, 1974), 255.

7. See especially Hans Frei, *The Identity of Jesus Christ: The Hermeneutical Bases of Dogmatic Theology* (Philadelphia: Fortress Press, 1975).

8. Richard B. Hays, *Echoes of Scripture in the Letters of Paul* (New Haven and London: Yale University Press, 1989), 66.

9. J. Louis Martyn, *History and Theology in the Fourth Gospel* (Nashville: Abingdon, 1968; 2d ed. 1979).

10. Hays, 183.

11. Gadamer suggests that *play* is a splendid metaphor for the presentation and re-presentation of art, *Truth and Method*, 91-99.

12. See Michael Fishbane, *Biblical Interpretation in Ancient Israel* (Oxford: Clarendon Press, 1985), 74-77.

13. A splendid corrective is Ellen Davis' fine book *Imagination Shaped: Old Testament Preaching in the Anglican Tradition* (Valley Forge: Trinity International, 1995). See, for instance, Lancelot Andrewes expanding on the story of the Three Magi (as T. S. Eliot would later expand on Andrewes in *The Journey of the Magi*). Davis points out both the vividness of the description and the fact that the description has a moral, theological point, p. 20.

14. Fishbane, 167-168.

15. Ibid., 285-286.

16. Ibid., 326.

17. I am persuaded by Lloyd Kittlaus' claim that the author of John's Gospel knew the Gospel of Mark though he did not rely on Mark's Gospel to nearly the extent that Matthew or Luke did. However, whether one accepts that thesis or not, it does seem evident that the author of John's Gospel knew some of the traditions that we find especially in Mark and sought to correct them according to his own theological perspective. Lloyd Kittlaus, "John and Mark: A Methodological Evaluation of Norman Perrin's Suggestion" in *Society of Biblical Literature 1979: Seminar Papers* (Atlanta: Scholars Press), 269-279.

18. Mark uses the Septuagint reading, which places *the voice* rather than *the way* in the wilderness; and Matthew follows him. Compare the NRSV's translation of the Hebrew Isaiah 40:3.

19. That this is the context for John's Gospel is argued helpfully by J. Louis Martyn, *History and Theology*.

Chapter 1: The World in Front of the Text

1. Paul Ricoeur is dealing with the interpretation of symbols, but his distinction works for the interpretation of larger texts as well. The discussion is found in *Freud and Philosophy: An Essay on Interpretation*, trans. Denis Savage (New Haven and London: Yale, 1970), 20-56.

2. Ricoeur, p. 27. See the whole discussion of retrieval and suspicion in Anthony C. Thistleton, *New Horizons in Biblical Hermeneutics: The Theory and Practice of Transforming Biblical Reading* (Grand Rapids: Zondervan, 1992), 344-378. For this quotation, see p. 347.

3. Ricoeur, "The Hermeneutical Function of Distanciation," in *Hermeneutics and the Human Sciences*, ed. and trans. John B. Thompson (Cambridge: Cambridge University Press, 1981), 143. The whole essay is on pp. 132-144.

4. The classic statement is "The Intentional Fallacy" by W. K. Wimsatt in *The Verbal Icon* (London: Methuen & Company, 1970), 2-18. This quotation is from p. 18. The original articles in the book were written between 1941–1952. Other "new critics" included Cleanth Brooks, Monroe Beardsley, and Robert Penn Warren.

5. Here the classic treatment is Cleanth Brooks "The Heresy of Paraphrase," in *The Well Wrought Urn* (New York: Harcourt, Brace & World, 1947), 192-214.

6. Robert Frost, *The Complete Poems* (London: Jonathan Cape, 1959), 250.

7. Among the early enthusiasts were Dan O. Via, *The Parables: Their Literary and Existential Dimension* (Philadelphia: Fortress, 1967); John

Dominic Crossan, *In Parables: The Challenge of the Historical Jesus* (New York: Harper & Row, 1973); and Norman Perrin, *Jesus and the Language of the Kingdom: Symbol and Metaphor in New Testament Interpretation* (Philadelphia: Fortress, 1976). See also Paul Ricoeur's splendid Rockefeller Chapel sermon, "Listening to the Parables of Jesus," in *The Philosophy of Paul Ricoeur: An Anthology of His Work*, ed. Charles E. Regan & David Stewart (Boston: Beacon Press, 1978), 239-245.

8. The classic works were Joachim Jeremias, *The Parables of Jesus* (New York: Scribner's, 1963); and C. H. Dodd, *The Parables of the Kingdom*, trans. S. H. Hooke (New York: Scribner's, 1972).

9. I would have to say that among these early literary critics of the parables, the heresy of paraphrase died a lot faster and harder than the intentional fallacy. We had lots of paragraphs on what a clever and intentional poet/storyteller our Lord turned out to be.

10. See, for instance, Jack Dean Kingsbury, *Matthew As Story* (Philadelphia: Fortress, 1986); David Rhoads and Donald Michie, *Mark As Story: An Introduction to the Narrative of a Gospel* (Philadelphia: Fortress, 1982); Robert Tannehill, *The Narratative Unity of Luke-Acts: A Literary Interpretation* (Philadelphia: Fortress, 1986); R. Alan Culpepper, *The Anatomy of the Fourth Gospel* (Philadelphia: Fortress, 1983–1987); and Robert Alter, *The Art of Biblical Narrative* (New York: Basic Books, 1984).

11. Kingsbury has paid special attention to this plot device in his studies of the Gospels.

12. E. M. Forster, *Aspects of the Novel* (New York: Harcourt, Brace, 1927, 1954), 67-78.

13. See Forster, 78.

14. Forster, 68.

15. Jack Miles, *God: A Biography* (New York: Random House, 1995).

16. For a discussion of how these first-person narratives function in Paul's writings, see David L. Bartlett, *The Shape of Scriptural Authority* (Philadelphia: Fortress, 1983), 119-125.

17. This also contrasts with the delight of many post-structuralists in finding things that don't fit; contradictions, fissures, and surprises.

18. See Kingsbury's *Conflict in Mark: Jesus, Authorities, Disciples* (Minneapolis: Fortress, 1989).

19. Robert Alter, "Sodom as Nexus: The Web of Design in Biblical Narrative," in Regina M. Schwartz *The Book and the Text: The Bible and Literary Theory* (Oxford and Cambridge: Basil Blackwell, 1990), 146-160.

20. See Alter, 149.

21. Ibid., 150. His emphasis.

22. Ibid., 157.

23. Ibid., 158-160. Alter makes it clear throughout this article that the shaping of Genesis and of the Hebrew Bible is not like the shaping of, say, *Tom Jones*, though Fielding, too, leaves plenty of room for—apparent—digression.

24. Robert M. Fowler, "Reader-Response Criticism: Figuring Mark's Reader," in *Mark and Method: New Approaches in Biblical Studies*, ed. Janice Capel Anderson and Stephen D. Moore (Minneapolis: Augsburg Fortress, 1992), 51. The article is on pp. 50-83.

25. For a discussion of the various kinds of "reader," see Robert M. Fowler, *Let the Reader Understand: Reader-Response Criticism and the Gospel of Mark* (Minneapolis: Fortress, 1991). As I understand ("read") Fowler, he wants a reader who is sufficiently open that the reading is shaped by the text, not just by the reader's prejudices or biorhythms. Stephen D. Moore also usefully reminds us that for the Gospels, for instance, the early "readers" were usually not "readers" but "hearers." See Moore, *Literary Criticism and the Gospels* (New Haven and London: Yale University Press, 1989), 84-86. The whole dynamic of the enterprise is different if it does not presuppose the book in front of me, my ability to flip forward and back through its pages. My guess is that for most contemporary Christians the story is again more often heard than read. Certainly preachers and lectors want to think about listener-response criticism.

26. See Fowler, *Let the Reader Understand*, 69-70; and *Loaves and Fishes: The Function of the Feeding Stories in the Gospel of Mark* (SBL Dissertation Series 54) (Chico: Scholars Press, 1981).

27. My own attempt to "hear" from the listener's perspective usually includes audiotaping the sermon sometime before I preach it, taking a few hours off from sermon preparation to listen to the sermon as if I were a member of the congregation and not a preacher.

28. Janice Capel Anderson and Stephen D. Moore, eds. *Mark and Method: New Approaches in Biblical Studies* (Minneapolis: Augsburg Fortress, 1992), 14-15.

29. A. K. M. Adam does a fine job of suggesting how deconstructive readers nonetheless continue to engage in discourse: "Deconstruction does not, after all, teach us that communication or knowledge or transcendence is impossible; it teaches us that these matters are awkwardly entangled in the various discourses." Adam, *What Is Postmodern Biblical Criticism?* (Minneapolis: Fortress, 1995), 31. My suspicion is that while this is a healthy reminder for preachers involved in the task of interpretation, we need to bring some closure to the wealth of possibilities before we begin to preach; preaching requires a certain amount of disentangling.

30. Stephen D. Moore, *Poststructuralism and the New Testament: Derrida and Foucault at the Foot of the Cross* (Minneapolis: Fortress, 1994), 62. The whole discussion of John 4 is found on pp. 43-64.

31. Moore, 62 n. 69.

32. See Adam, 47.

33. See Stephen Greenblatt, *Renaissance Self-Fashioning* (Chicago and London: University of Chicago Press, 1980), 24-25; and *Shakespearean Negotiations: The Circulation of Social Energy in Renaissance England* (Berkeley and Los Angeles: University of California Press, 1988), 129-132. Preachers will note the appropriate hermeneutics of homiletical suspicion that Greenblatt exercises regarding Latimer's sermon illustration: "It is not only that Latimer lives his life as if it were material for the stories he will tell in his sermons, but that the actions he reports are comprehensible only if already fashioned into a story" (195 n. 25).

34. Greenblatt, *Learning to Curse* (New York and London: Routledge, 1990), 80-82.

35. Sometimes there is a kind of Marxist subtext here; nothing is valued that does not finally have economic value. Sometimes that claim is not so evident.

36. See the haunting Epilogue in Greenblatt's *Renaissance Self-Fashioning*, 255-257, and Miller's self-revealing, self-concealing recollection of his first reading of *David Copperfield*, in *The Novel and the Police* (Berkeley, Los Angeles, and London: University of California Press), 194-195. On the use of anecdote in new historical writings, see Joel Fineman, "The History of the Anecdote: Fiction and Fiction" in *The New Historicism*, ed. H. Aram Veeser (New York and London: Routledge, 1989), 49-76.

37. For a helpful discussion, see Adam, *What Is Postmodern Biblical Criticism?* 47-58. For further discussion and an example, see Mary Ann Tolbert, "The Gospel in Greco-Roman Culture," in *The Book and the Text: The Bible and Literary Theory*, ed. Regina M. Schwartz (Oxford and Cambridge: Basil Blackwell, 1990), 259-275.

38. Dale Martin, *Slavery as Salvation: The Metaphor of Slavery in Pauline Christianity* (New Haven and London: Yale University Press, 1990), xiv.

39. See Martin, 2.

40. Ibid., xiv.

41. Ibid., xx.

42. See Martin's discussion, 63-68.

43. Martin, 68.

44. Ibid., 51-59.

45. Ibid., 145-146.

46. There is a very good discussion of canonical criticism by Mary C. Callaway in *To Each Their Own Meaning: An Introduction to Biblical Criticisms and Their Application*, ed. Stephen R. Haynes and Steven L. McKenzie (Louisville: Westminster/John Knox, 1993), 121-134.

47. In fact, Brevard S. Childs handles this issue in a very nuanced way in *The New Testament as Canon: An Introduction* (Philadelphia: Fortress, 1985), 141-142. He acknowledges both that chapter 21 probably represents a "later" addition to the Gospel and that it shapes the Gospel's canonical function both internally and in relation to other New Testament texts.

48. See Childs, *The New Testament as Canon*, 419-427.

49. Letter from Childs, October 26, 1997. Childs also suggests, in a way obviously congenial to the concerns of this book, that the farther a method of biblical studies is separated from canonical concerns the harder it is for preachers to draw on that method to declare Scripture, or preaching, as the word of God. See also Childs, *Biblical Theology of the Old and New Testaments: Theological Reflection on the Christian Bible* (Minneapolis: Fortress, 1992), 71.

50. Childs' letter. This last example is a nice instance of how Childs' approach differs from much of historical-critical work, which is often engaged in showing how little Acts provides an accurate guide to the "real" Paul, who wrote at least the "real" letters. For further discussion, see Childs, *The New Testament as Canon*, 238-289.

51. Childs, *Biblical Theology*, 73-74. Childs also wants to make clear that contemporary interpreters are not bound by canonical principles to interpret the Old Testament only and always as New Testament writers did. When that happens "the Old Testament has . . . lost its vertical, existential dimension which as Scripture of the church continues to bear its own witness within the context of the Christian Bible."

52. See Callaway, 131.

53. I am grateful to Professor Childs for a very helpful letter clarifying for me the relationship of his canonical questions to the issue of the life of communities of faith—historically and at the present.

54. Childs, *The Book of Exodus: A Critical, Theological Commentary*, The Old Testament Library (Philadelphia: Westminster, 1974), 51-71.

55. Childs, *Exodus*, 74-75.

56. Ibid., 76.

57. Ibid., 82.

58. For a thorough and largely persuasive study of the way this passage interprets the Old Testament, see Peder Borgen, *Bread from Heaven: An Exegetical Study of the Concept of Manna in the Gospel of John and the Works of Philo*, supplement to *Novum Testamentum* 10 (Leiden: E. J. Brill, 1965); and Wayne A. Meeks, *The Prophet-King: Moses Traditions and Johannine Christology*, supplement to *Novum Testamentum* 14 (Leiden: E. J. Brill, 1967).

59. Rudolf Bultmann, *The Gospel of John*, trans., G. R. Beasley-Murray (Philadelphia: Westminster, 1975), 234-237.

Chapter 2: The World Behind the Text

1. Wayne A. Meeks, *The First Urban Christians: The Social World of the Apostle Paul* (New Haven and London: Yale University Press, 1983), 2.

2. Ibid.

3. Meeks, 73.

4. We shall see that other social critics of the text move more quickly and more zealously to embrace particular sociological or anthropological models.

5. Meeks, 73.

6. Meeks, 141.

7. All of these suggestions are in Meeks, 191.

8. Gail O'Day, "Jeremiah 9:22-23 and 1 Corinthians 1:26-31: A Study in Intertextuality," *JBL1 109* (Summer 1990), 259-267.

9. Note that according to Meeks' reading of the whole body of Pauline letters the first reading is more likely; some may have been wealthy and powerful and of noble birth, but probably "not many."

10. For a good discussion of the weak and strong as status/economic categories, with appropriate cautionary notes, see Abraham J. Malherbe, *Social Aspects of Early Christianity* (Philadelphia: Fortress, 1983), 71-91.

11. But should the lowly also kneel? See chapter 3.

12. See Malherbe, 20.

13. Ibid., 23.

14. Ibid., 25.

15. Ibid., 26-27. For a fuller discussion of Paul and the Thessalonian Christians, see Malherbe, *Paul and the Thessalonians: The Philosophic Tradition of Pastoral Care* (Philadelphia: Fortress, 1987).

16. Peter Lampe, *Die stadtrömischen Christen in den ersten beiden Jahrhunderten* (Tübingen: J. C. B. Mohr [Paul Siebeck], 1987).

17. For a further discussion of this passage in the context of issues of church unity, see David L. Bartlett, *Romans: Westminster Bible Companion* (Louisville: Westminster/John Knox, 1995).

18. Robert R. Wilson, *Sociological Approaches to the Old Testament* (Philadelphia: Fortress, 1984).

19. Ibid., 7.

20. Ibid., 79. Also see *Prophecy and Society in Ancient Israel* (Philadelphia: Fortress, 1980), 250-251.

21. Jerome Neyrey, *An Ideology of Revolt: John's Christology in Social-Science Perspective* (Philadelphia: Fortress, 1988). This is helpfully summarized in Urban C. von Wahlde, "Community in Conflict: The History and Social Context of the Johannine Community," *Interpretation* XLIX, 4 (October, 1995), 379-388; esp. 385-387.

22. L. Michael White, "Crisis Management and Boundary Maintenance" in *Social History of the Matthean Communities: Cross-Disciplinary Approaches*, ed. David L. Balch (Minneapolis: Fortress, 1991), 211-242. The quotation is from pp. 222-223.

23. White, 238-242.

24. Dale Martin adds another helpful cautionary note: "The problem with the term 'model,' however, is that it may refer to a classification system as abstract, rigid, and universalizing as Mary Douglas's 'group-grid' construction, or to a conceptual construction as culturally specific, freely used, and content-oriented as patron-client systems or societal perceptions of honor and shame. Few historical critics, if any, doubt the usefulness of knowledge about ancient patron-client structures for interpretation of early Christianity. Many scholars, on the other hand, have found the group-grid mode to be too rigid or uninteresting, if not downright incomprehensible, when applied to New Testament texts." "Social Scientific Criticism" in *To Each Its Own Meaning*, eds. Steven L. McKenzie and Stephen R. Haynes (Louisville: Westminster/John Knox, 1993), 107.

25. David Rensberger, *Johannine Faith and Liberating Community* (Philadelphia: Westminster, 1988), 28.

26. Ibid., 78-81. This interpretation depends in part on the (literary) strategy of reading the eucharistic passages as "displaced" from the usual position in the Lord's Supper and therefore as a kind of pair with the "farewell" discourses that Jesus delivers at the Lord's Supper instead.

27. I have also noted what others have recently much mentioned, that those looking for social-scientific models for biblical study seem to be moving more and more to analogies drawn from anthropology rather than sociology.

28. Norman Gottwald, *The Tribes of Yahweh: A Sociology of the Religion of Liberated Israel, 1250–1050 B.C.E.* (Maryknoll, N.Y.: Orbis, 1979), 701. The italics are his.

29. See chapter 1 discussion on Childs' reading of Exodus 3, pp. 67-68.

30. Gottwald, 321.

31. Ibid., 508. It needs to be noted that Gottwald does not set out to write a commentary or a guide for preaching Exodus, but a historical and social reconstruction. He does, of course, give some clues to his theological take on all this.

32. William R. Herzog, *Parables as Subversive Speech: Jesus as Pedagogue of the Oppressed* (Louisville: Westminster/John Knox, 1994).

33. Ibid., 79-97.

34. Ched Myers, *Binding the Strong Man: A Political Reading of Mark's Story of Jesus* (Maryknoll, N.Y.: Orbis, 1988), 11.

35. Ibid., 322.

36. Wilson, 29. See also my review of John Gager's early work on social scientific study of the New Testament in *Zygon*, XIII/2 (June 1978), 109-122.

Chapter 3: Our World and the Text

1. Ched Myers, *Binding the Strong Man: A Political Reading of Mark's Story of Jesus* (Maryknoll, N.Y.: Orbis, 1988), 7-8.

2. Of course this concern has not been absent from other modes of interpretation, especially reader-response criticism, though the strategy there has most often been to posit an ideal reader—either a reader contemporary with the biblical book or a reader contemporary with us. Reader-response criticism does not usually ask about the politics or social location or denominational affiliation of its "reader." See chapter 1.

3. There is also no reason in principle why a perspectival reading of a text might be undertaken from a social location indebted to and loyal to the (almost absolute) values of the free market.

4. See our discussion of Ricoeur in chapter 1. The actual phrase "retrieval" may be from David Tracy, who treats both kinds of hermeneutics in *The Analogical Imagination* (New York: Crossroad, 1981). See especially p. 190, n. 71.

5. Fernando F. Segovia and Mary Ann Tolbert, eds., *Reading from This Place*, vol. 1; *Social Location and Biblical Interpretation in the United States*, vol. 2; and *Social Location and Biblical Interpretation in Global Perspective* (Minneapolis: Fortress, 1995).

6. Segovia, in his article "And They Began to Speak in Other Tongues," in *Reading from This Place*, vol. 1, 29. The whole article is on pp. 1-32.

7. For a somewhat different list of our biases, see Daniel Patte, "The Contextual Character of Male, European-American Critical Exegesis," in *Reading from This Place*, vol. 1, 35-73.

8. Paulo Fernando Carneiro de Andrade, "Reading the Bible in the Ecclesial Base Communities of Latin America: The Meaning of Social Context," in *Reading from This Place*, vol. 2, 239. The whole article is found on pp. 237-249.

9. Ibid., 241.

10. Carlos Mesters, *Defenseless Flower: A New Reading of the Bible*, trans. Francis McDonagh (Maryknoll, N.Y.: Orbis, 1989).

11. See Mesters, 5-10.

12. Ibid., 13-22; see here also the article by Andrade.

13. Ibid., 19.

14. Ibid., 33. The whole discussion of letter and spirit includes attention to the ways in which the church fathers interpreted texts allegorically, that is, spiritually. See pp. 20-34.

15. de Andrade, in *Reading from This Place*, vol. 2, pp. 237-249. The quotation is from p. 247.

16. I am not in a good position to judge whether some Latin American Chris-

tians overvalue Marx; I am quite convinced that most American Christians undervalue him and use the collapse of the Soviet Union as a quick excuse to stop worrying about the ways in which economic interests affect ideologies and theologies, including our own.

17. Ernesto Cardenal, *The Gospel in Solentiname*, vol. 1, trans. Donald D. Walsh (Maryknoll, N.Y.: Orbis, 1976).

18. Cardenal, 29-30.

19. Phyllis Trible, *God and the Rhethoric of Sexuality (Overtures to Biblical Theology)* (Philadelphia: Fortress, 1978), 16.

20. Ibid., 90.

21. Elisabeth Schüssler Fiorenza, *In Memory of Her: A Feminist Theological Reconstruction of Christian Origins* (New York: Crossroad, 1984), 131-132.

22. See Schüssler Fiorenza, 161. Chapter 6 of the book cites the evidence and spells out the implications.

23. For Schüssler Fiorenza's description of an appropriate feminist methodology, see "The Will to Choose or Reject: Continuing our Critical Work," in *Feminist Interpretation of the Bible*, ed. Letty M. Russell (Philadelphia: Westminster, 1985), 125-136. This quotation is from p. 130.

24. Ringe, Sharon, *Luke: Westminster Bible Companion* (Louisville: Westminster/John Knox Press, 1995), 11.

25. Ibid., 283-285.

26. Ibid., 12.

27. Antoinette Wire, "1 Corinthians," in *Searching the Scriptures*, vol. 2: *A Feminist Commentary*, ed. Elisabeth Schüssler Fiorenza (New York: Crossroad, 1994), pp. 153-194. The commentary on this section is found on pp. 185-189, and the quotation on pp. 187-188.

28. Ibid., 188. For a fuller reconstruction of the social situation of women in the Corinthian church, see Antoinette Wire, *The Corinthian Women Prophets: A Reconstruction Through Paul's Rhetoric* (Minneapolis: Fortress, 1990).

29. Carol A. Newsom and Sharon H. Ringe, eds., *The Women's Bible Commentary* (Louisville: Westminster/John Knox, 1992), 50.

30. Howard Thurman, *Jesus and the Disinherited* (Nashville: Abingdon Press, 1949), pp. 30-31, quoted in Renita J. Weems, "African American Women and the Bible," in *Stony the Road We Trod: African American Biblical Interpretation*, ed., Cain Hope Felder (Minneapolis: Fortress, 1991), 61-62. The whole article is on pp. 57-77.

31. Renita J. Weems, "African American Women and the Bible," in Felder, *Stony the Road We Trod*, 62.

32. On this see Lloyd Lewis, "An African American Appraisal of the Philemon-Paul-Onesimus Triangle," in Felder, *Stony the Road We Trod*, 233.

33. See Preface to James and Jude and to the Revelation of St. John in Mar-

tin Luther, *Works*, vol. 35, ed. E. Theodore Bachmann (Philadelphia: Fortress, 1960), 395-399.

34. Copher, "The Black Presence in the Old Testament" in Felder, *Stony the Road We Trod*, 146-164.

35. Lewis, in Felder, *Stony the Road We Trod*, 232-246. The quotation is from p. 246.

36. Abraham Smith, "A Second Step in African Biblical Interpretation: A Generic Reading Analysis of Acts 8:26-40," in *Reading from This Place*, vol. 1, 214. The whole article is found on pp. 213-228. In this sense Smith does what we will urge in the final chapter of this book—he broadens the notion of the appropriation of texts or stories to acknowledge communal listening.

37. Smith, 214-215.

38. Smith, 228.

39. Philadelphia: Westminster Press. I need to acknowledge how much this book helped open my eyes to other perspectives on Scripture. As a companion piece North American pastors should read Brown's reflections on what the gospel means to the relatively affluent Presbyterians he served as interim pastor in Palo Alto; see "A Funny Thing Happened on the Way to the Pulpit" in *The Christian Century*, 111 (July 27-Aug. 3, 1994), 723-724.

40. Brown, 13-14.

41. The whole discussion of this passage is found on 127-141.

42. For a different reading of the "nations" in the story, see our discussion of Ulrich Luz in this chapter.

43. Sharon Ringe, "Solidarity and Contextuality: Readings of Matthew 18:21-35," in *Reading from This Place*, vol. 1, 200-201. The whole article is found on pp. 199-212.

44. Ibid., 208.

45. Ibid., 209.

46. Stephen Breck Reid, *Listening In: A Multicultural Reading of the Psalms* (Nashville: Abingdon, 1997), 104.

47. Reid, 62.

48. Notice that as one move in his multifaceted interpretive strategy Reid here practices the kind of canonical readings that Brevard Childs advocates.

49. Reid, 67-69.

50. In this class, those who saw themselves as "outsiders" were Reid's "mob at the gates" (see p. 8), primarily the African Americans, and those who saw themselves as the insiders were the Euro-Americans. Other members of the class, African and Hispanic, had slightly different slants on the story.

51. That is not to say that no reading could be wrong. In this case the text supports both interpretations.

52. Ulrich Luz, "The Final Judgment (Matt. 25:31-46): An Exercise in 'History of Influence' Exegesis," in David R. Bauer and Mark Alan Powell, eds. *Treasures New and Old: Contributions to Matthean Studies* (SBL Symposium Series Number One) (Atlanta: Scholars Press, 1996), 271-310. The quotation is from p. 271. Luz notes that the method has much in common with reader-response criticism, but it studies the response of real readers (not ideal ones) and does so across ages and cultures (pp. 272-273).

53. See Luz, 273.

54. Ibid., 273-280.

55. Ibid., 280-284.

56. For my own run at this kind of reading, complete with homiletical implications, see "Exegesis of Matthew 25:31-46," *Foundations* 19 (1976), 211-213.

57. Luz, 284-286. Luz says the reason for the emergence of this interpretation, unlike the other two, "does not lie in the fact that this interpretation corresponds to any specific needs of the present day, but simply in the fact that it is exegetically strong" (p. 286). My own reading of the history of interpretation would suggest that it will take a later generation of scholars to see what interests—in addition to exegetical care—may lie behind this move, interests that we are in no position to discern.

58. See Luz, 286-308.

59. Ibid., 305.

60. He does acknowledge this perspective on p. 276, but the major thrust of the essay stresses the readers' placement among the astonished sheep and goats, not among the least. I'm simply saying that the text isn't the only thing that determines how I hear the text, or where I place myself in the story.

61. See Luz, 308-309.

62. Ibid., 310.

63. Ibid.

64. I have argued elsewhere that we all have some principles of interpretation—a canon within the canon, a central motif that illumines other motifs, our picture of Jesus, our understanding of the scope of God's love. But we constantly test these against the specific texts that may broaden, stretch, or even disconfirm what we thought was so central. See David L. Bartlett, *The Shape of Scriptural Authority* (Philadelphia: Fortress, 1983), 140-146.

65. If you are too young to know what that means, then this illustration is lost on you.

Chapter 4: Historical Criticism Revisited

1. Krister Stendahl, "Biblical Theology, Contemporary," in *The Interpreter's Dictionary of the Bible*, vol. 1, ed. George Arthur Buttrick, et al. (Nashville: Abingdon, 1962), 418-431.

2. Stendahl, 422.

3. Contrast Rudolf Bultmann's commentary *The Gospel of John* (trans. G. R. Beasley-Murray, et al. [Philadelphia: Westminster, 1971]) with R. Alan Culpepper's *The Anatomy of the Fourth Gospel: A Study in Literary Design* (Philadelphia: Fortress, 1983). Bultmann seeks to explain disjunctions in the text by attention to a putative history of the sources behind the text. Culpepper reads the text as text, apparent disjunctions and all. Nonetheless, Bultmann time and again provides a reading of the text that seems perspicacious as a reading of John and fruitful as a resource for preaching.

4. See chapter 2, pp. 91-93.

5. See chapter 1, p. 37ff.

6. Walter Wink, "The Bankruptcy of the Biblical Critical Paradigm" in The *Bible in Human Transformation: Toward a New Paradigm of Bible Study* (Philadelphia: Fortress, 1973), 1-15.

7. See Stephen D. Moore, "Deconstructive Criticism," in *Mark and Method: New Approaches in Biblical Studies*, Janice Capel Anderson and Stephen D. Moore, eds. (Minneapolis: Fortress, 1992), 84-102.

8. See chapter 3, p. 118.

9. *Form and Function of the Pauline Thanksgivings* (Berlin: Töpelmann, 1939).

10. See J. Louis Martyn, *History and Theology in the Fourth Gospel*, 2d ed., (Nashville: Abingdon, 1979) and "Glimpses into the History of the Johannine Community," in *The Gospel of John in Christian History: Essays for Interpreters* (New York: Paulist Press, 1978), 90-121. For a rich reading of the Nicodemus story that relies in part on Martyn, see David Rensberger, *Johannine Faith and Liberating Community* (Philadelphia: Westminster, 1988), 37-52.

11. See chapter 2, pp. 85-86.

12. Patrick D. Miller, *They Cried to the Lord: The Form and Theology of Biblical Prayer* (Minneapolis: Fortress, 1994), 141.

13. Miller, 173. See also p. 184 and P. D. Miller, *Interpreting the Psalms* (Philadelphia: Fortress, 1986), 100-108.

14. Indeed this is one model for preaching that Henry H. Mitchell advocates in *Celebration and Experience* (Nashville: Abingdon, 1990); see especially chapter 4.

15. Harold W. Attridge, *The Epistle to the Hebrews* (Hermeneia) (Philadelphia: Fortress, 1989), 273-277.

16. Paulo Fernando Carneiro de Andrade, "Reading the Bible in the Ecclesial Base Communities of Latin America," in *Reading from this Place*, vol. 2, Fernando F. Segovia and Mary Ann Tolbert, eds. (Minneapolis: Fortress, 1995), 240-241. The whole article is found on pp. 237-249.

17. C. H. Dodd, *The Apostolic Preaching and Its Developments* (London: Hodder & Stoughton, 1936).

18. Notice how many different (homiletical?) endings we have for the parable of the dishonest steward, each a kind of attempt to preach it for some community situation. See Luke 16:1-10; I suspect v. 8*a* is the end of the early parable and that vv. 8*b*, 9, and 10 are all later homiletical applications.

19. David Buttrick, *Homiletic: Moves and Structures* (Philadelphia: Fortress, 1987), 276-277.

20. See John P. Meier, *A Marginal Jew: Rethinking the Historical Jesus* (New York: Doubleday, 1991).

21. Gerd Theissen, *Psychological Aspects of Pauline Theology*, trans. John P. Galvin (Philadelphia: Fortress, 1987); Robin Scroggs, "The Heuristic Value of a Psychoanalytic Model in the Interpretation of Pauline Theology," in Scroggs, *The Text and the Times* (Minneapolis: Fortress, 1993), 125-150; and Wink, *The Bible in Human Transformation*.

22. Wayne A. Meeks, *The Origins of Christian Morality: The First Two Centuries* (New Haven: Yale University Press, 1993); and Victor Paul Furnish, *The Moral Teaching of Paul* (Nashville: Abingdon, 1979).

23. See Thomas W. Ogletree, *The Use of the Bible in Christian Ethics: A Constructive Essay* (Philadelphia: Fortress, 1983).

24. See, for example, John Howard Yoder, *The Politics of Jesus: Vicit Agnus Noster*, 2d ed. (Grand Rapids: Eerdmans, 1994); and Stanley Hauerwas, *A Community of Character: Toward a Constructive Social Ethic* (Notre Dame: University of Notre Dame Press, 1981).

25. Some preachers who helped me think about this section of the book suggested that we expand the range of issues that biblical/cultural studies might mediate—especially attention to the demands of a technical (and high-tech) world, and the challenges posed by "New Age" spirituality.

26. A distinction I owe to William Sloane Coffin, Jr., who owes it to Arthur Miller. See Miller, *Incident at Vichy* (New York: Bantam, 1967), 107.